Praise

'This book will equip you with
charge of your life and play your A-game so that you
can make a meaningful impact in this world.'
— **Simon Alexander Ong, author of** *Energize:*
Make the most of every moment

'Totally on point! Everything outlined by Baiju is
both relevant and important; to sum up it's about
your Vision, Values and Velocity.'
— **Ketan Makwana, Co-Chair and Founder of**
Seventy7 Ventures

'Following on from *Change Your Game*, this book
provides the perfect companion for you to play your
A-game. When you make any changes there will
always be excitement, as well as challenges. Baiju
has provided a framework to help you deal with
the challenges you face when you are upping your
game, with the tools to be more consistent with your
A-game. A really inspiring read that will improve your
mindset, give you a clear strategy and enable you to
be more consistent and persistent with your actions.'
— **Daniel Priestley, bestselling author of**
Entrepreneur Revolution, Oversubscribed
and *24 Assets*

'Sometimes we can just get so bogged down in our
lives we forget to enjoy the journey. Baiju Solanki is
at the top of his game, and this book gives actionable
takeaways to transform your mindset and results.'
— **Alison Edgar MBE, author, speaker and**
entrepreneur, AKA The Entrepreneur's
Godmother

'This book will take you from playing the victim in your own story to getting out of your way and playing full-out in the story you now choose for yourself. No more excuses, no more allowing life to happen to you, no more wondering just how you ended up so damn busy all the time, and no more allowing habits to creep into your life, adding to the stress of every day. Watch the magic happen when you apply Baiju's game rules to your life. The next level of your life is just a few chapters away. What are you waiting for?'
    — **Jennifer Louise, Founder and CEO of Obsessions Salon and The Successful Salon Club**

'I am a man who likes a no-nonsense approach; *Play Your Game* gives you the strategy without the nonsense. Practical proven methods ensure you maximise your chances of winning your game and staying on track.'
    — **Spencer Lodge, investor, business strategist and award-winning podcast host**

'This book is a fantastic guide to anyone looking to move forward in life. Not only does it pull together several tried-and-tested theories, but it also gives the reader clear, actionable steps to take their life to the next level.'
    — **Carl Reader, entrepreneur, speaker and author of bestseller *Boss It: Control your time, your income and your life***

To Jane, Hope you enjoy the book Baiju x

PLAY YOUR GAME

Take Radical Action and
Win the Leadership &
Entrepreneurial Game

BAIJU SOLANKI

R^ethink

First published in Great Britain in 2022
by Rethink Press (www.rethinkpress.com)

© Copyright Baiju Solanki

Author photograph: Sharron Goodyear, www.sharrongoodyear.com, @SharronGoodyear

Contents

Introduction

When I wrote my previous book, *Change Your Game*, I wanted to show people that entrepreneurship was not about business, but about mindset and behaviours. *Change Your Game* was about how you look at your life and your business. What small changes can you make in terms of mindset, strategy and action?

Now, in *Play Your Game*, we are on the court and ready to play. We're going to play smart, and we're going to have fun. We will play with intentionality. But first, we have to get unstuck.

This book explains how, once you change your game, to sustain it and play your A-game full-out each day, without burning out. It gives you the tools to ensure the bad moments stay as moments, and don't become bad days. Starting something is easy; keeping it going is the hard part.

This book is for people who:

- Want to feel free

- Want to play full-out

- Want more from life

- Want to feel in control

- Want to have a structure that allows success and fun

This book is for entrepreneurs, business owners, leaders and athletes, but the principles can be applied in all areas of life. When you adopt an entrepreneurial mindset and behaviours, anyone can change their life, especially those feeling like they could achieve more.

Before you get into this book, I recommend you assess how strong your game currently is. I have created a free assessment tool you can use to determine how effective you are as an entrepreneur and leader, which you can find at: https://ChangeYourGameScorecard.com

There are sound structures you can implement set out here and in *Change Your Game*. In addition, *Win Your Game Planner* will help with your discipline on a daily, weekly and monthly basis to ensure you stay on top of your A-game.

My transformation: committed and coachable

In December 2018, my life looked great – from the outside. I had just published *Change Your Game*, and, following my marriage breakdown and a lot of self-reflection and healing, I had a clear vision for my business and my life.

However, I wasn't entirely happy with myself, something was missing. When you become more self-aware and see that actually you don't need most of the things that society tells us are necessary for happiness, you start to question everything. This is empowering.

I decided to go on a yoga retreat to India, to reflect on my life and identify why I wasn't happy and what was missing. There, I realised it was my health that was the issue, and how I was feeling on a day-to-day basis. I wasn't full of energy. I was tired a lot and woke up with aches and pains. This affected my productivity, which in turn impacted my social life and the results I was seeing in my business. I had to address my physical health to improve my mental health and lead me to happiness. I was willing to work on myself in order to become happier and more successful. I took the view that a happy and healthy person would be more successful, that happiness and health breed success, not the other way round.

Back then I was a little bit overweight. I felt lethargic, low on energy and I lacked discipline with food and exercise. When I did do or eat something healthy, it was very much a tick-box exercise rather than intentional behaviour. I knew for sure that I was not interested in a fad diet; I wanted to completely change my lifestyle. A few friends of mine were seeking a similar transformation. I contacted the organisation they were working with while I was in India and said, 'I don't want a diet, I don't just want to do some exercise, I want a transformation.'

My aim was to lose 10 kilos in six months. Within three months, I had done it. I was eating sensibly, was disciplined in my exercise and let myself be coached, not questioning anything they told me to do. Once I'd met my target, I thought I was done, but my coach pointed out that in my business I encourage people to push their limits and push outside their comfort zone to see what's possible. I thought, 'Okay, I'll take on the challenge.' Over the next six months, I saw the biggest personal growth of my life. It gave me focus, discipline and a sense of direction. Although I was focused on improving my physical health, the impact on my mental health, my business and my relationships, was huge. All of this discipline in my personal life trickled into my focus on my work. I understood what I needed to do so that I and everybody around me benefited. Ultimately, I achieved my transformation because I was committed, I wanted it and I was coachable.

I realised that playing my 'A-game' was about self-discipline, being focused and leaning into what I needed to do. It wasn't about anybody else. This book shows you how to play your A-game, which requires you to be coachable, disciplined and focused. All of these things are completely within your control. My transformation showed me that when you decide *who* you want to be and start living as that person, the world sees it and gives you what you need.

The Change Your Game model

When you look at successful people, whether in sport, business or any other context, what they all have in common is not what they *want* but the way they *are*. Notably, they:

- Think differently

- Behave differently

- Deal with failure differently

- Deal with challenges differently

- Deal with life in a whole different way

Everything you need to know to play your A-game is in this book, but if you haven't already, reading *Change Your Game* will provide solid foundations and make the insights of this book even more impactful.

In *Change Your Game*, I introduced the CYG model:

The model focuses on three areas:

1. **The Inner Game**: All your thoughts, feelings and emotions relate to your inner game – this is how you make decisions, the way you view the world, the people you trust and why you trust them, how you deal with failure, what you are afraid of, and how resilient you are.

2. **The Game Plan**: This is your overall strategy and roadmap for the life you desire. What does the big picture look like? What is your strategy? This is about more than having plans to achieve your goals; it's about looking at the bigger picture and understanding where individual components fit in.

3. **The Outer Game**: The size of the action you take is not important. If you take a small action consistently, every day, you will reap far greater rewards than if you take big actions every now and then but then do nothing for long periods of time.

Change Your Game explained what game you want to be playing. Now, it's time to play. *Play Your Game* sets out the actions you need to take within an overall strategic approach.

This book is split into two parts. Part 1: Prepare For The Game consists of five sections where I talk you through what happens when you choose to play your A-game and shift your mindset: the opportunities that will present themselves, the inevitable resistance that will occur, the reality of what is happening and how you can respond.

Part 2: Playing On The Court is all about playing, about being on the court. It's how you show up for others, how you deal with different perspectives and the power of accountability and consistent, persistent actions. When you start this journey and see the impact it has, there is no turning back. It requires a certain attitude that can be seen as selfish, but this is not the case. Your pursuit of excellence and growth cannot be selfish, as when you take care of yourself, the world gets the best of you. Many people take care of others before themselves. I used to be like this. The problem is, this way, nobody – not you, nor the people you care for – gets the best of you. Play your A-game, and everyone wins.

This book will guide you, empower you and allow you to embrace others along the way. *Play Your Game* will give you the formula for how to play your A-game. You will be in flow, your actions will feel effortless, you will feel unbeatable. When confronted with a challenge you will find a way to turn it into an opportunity.

Enjoy the ride, your A-game is not far away – you are ready.

PART 1
PREPARE FOR THE GAME

In Part 1, we go deeper into the principles of the inner game, as you prepare to play your A-game. This is your chance to prepare for the game ahead and condition your internal dialogue to ensure your actions come from a place of total control. Your mindset leads your preparation to play, how you interpret and respond to what is ahead of you, how you take control of the play and how you respond to the movements of the game, adjusting as the play move forwards. You control the game.

The Foundation

This section is about the principles of the inner game and creating the space to play it. Deciding to play by your own rules, to take control and be as successful and happy as you can be, takes a particular state of mind. The foundation we must build first is the new mindset you need to adopt.

1. No more excuses

Between where you are now and where you want to be are excuses. More excuses mean a bigger distance to travel and a harder journey. You can choose to live with excuses or without them. Most excuses are based on assumptions that we disguise as truths and they keep you playing a small game. Some of the reasons people are tempted by excuses are:

- They keep you safe
- You won't ever fail
- You don't have to take action
- You can live without ever feeling uncertain

Excuses only lead to more excuses. Can you challenge yourself to think of reasons instead? Reasons allow you to be more strategic. You can map out the what, when and how to make something work. Excuses root you in the past, convincing you you're not ready, not good enough or that nothing will change.

An exercise you can do right now – no excuses – is to get a piece of paper and write down all the excuses you have for not creating the life, business, relationship you want now. Then, for every excuse, come up with a reason *to* do the thing you're excusing, a reason strong enough to trump the excuse.

For example, in *Change Your Game* I talked about all the excuses I had for not leaving my well-paid job and creating the business and life I wanted. Excuses like:

- I'm not ready
- I'm not good enough

- I'm not financially stable enough

These were my excuses for why I hadn't done it; next I came up with reasons why I should:

- I may never be ready but I have to start somewhere

- I will never know what's out there unless I try

- I could change my financial situation for the better

As I mentioned, most excuses we make up to keep ourselves safe and to not take action. The one genuine excuse I had was the last one, my concern about financial stability. The other two were made up to enable me to stay small and not take any action, consumed by thoughts of 'what if'. How many of your excuses fall into this category? When you start to analyse all your excuses, you will find probably only a handful of genuine reasons you can't do something. The others are all based on your opinions about the world you're living in – in other words, they're BS. The more truthful you are here in identifying your excuses, the bigger the impact this book and the decisions you go on to make will be. Note the date and time – this is the moment you finally eliminated all your BS excuses and now have a list of reasons to move forward. Now you can make a plan. This book will help you do just that.

Get out of your own way. I promise, if you do this now, your life will never be the same.

2. When life happens

'Life happens' to all of us. You need to be organised to limit the impact when it does. Social media can give the impression that life only happens to us and no one else has it as bad. They do. Life happens to everyone, all the time – it's happening right now. If you are reading or listening to this book in public, have a look around. All these people have stuff going on. Some have bigger challenges than you, some have smaller ones. Some are coping better than others. Some have given up; some are determined to overcome their barriers. Some have the tools, some do not; some don't even know where to find the tools. Some know exactly what to do but still won't do it. This is not a judgement, but a fact.

Where do you sit? The fact that you are reading this book means you are determined to address your challenges, you have the tools you need, you want to learn and, more importantly, take action. That's a great place to be. This book will be part of your journey.

A simple formula captures the essence of all that we'll talk about in *Play Your Game*: the Freedom Formula.

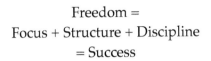

Freedom =
Focus + Structure + Discipline
= Success

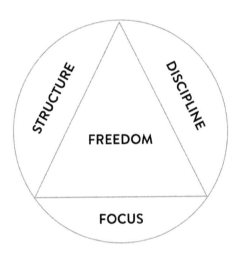

There is a common perception that highly successful people have no problems and life doesn't happen to them like it does to us. Not true. Life happens to you whether you are successful or not, rich or poor, young or old. In this book, I will explain how you can regain focus when life happens. What I mean by this is the things that we don't expect or plan for that throw our world into chaos. Things like:

- Job loss

- Accidents

- Money issues

- A family illness

- Relationship problems

You know the kind of stuff I mean. It happens to all of us. The difference is how we react or, better still, respond. Depending on how organised, together, calm, aligned – whatever you want to call it – you are, you will either *react* or *respond* to life events.

When you *react*, this is usually emotionally driven and without any thought. When you *respond*, you come from a place of reason, empowerment and together-ness, and are able to deal with life better.

Life is always going to happen; the key is to prepare now. Too many people wait until the proverbial hits the fan. In that mode, you are reactive, playing catch-up, panicking even. Look to develop focus, structure and discipline when you are in a good place, so that when you're not, you are at least more in control. When you love what you do, when you find balance in the areas of life that you have control over, you will be in a better place overall to deal with adversity. This book will help.

3. No compromise

When you play your A-game you don't compromise on your standards. Humans like to please, but often we do so at the cost of our values and standards. This needn't be the case – you can have it all.

Do you live to your own principles or those of others? Do you compromise on things so you don't upset people, or allow their way of doing things to become the norm?

CASE STUDY: HARPREET CHANA

I met Harpreet Chana at a networking event where I was speaking. She was working full time in the corporate world within the pharmacy industry, but she had a vision of establishing her own business supporting mental health through 'mental wealth' and self-leadership in healthcare, drawing on her own challenges around mental wellness and leadership while in a demanding senior national role.

Harpreet joined the Change Your Game Accelerator while still in her corporate position, with the aim of building her 'side hustle' business and then leaving on her own terms.

She had a young family, was the main breadwinner and felt stuck. What was evident working with Harpreet was her no-nonsense determination to achieve her dream and do what she wanted to do, even with all the challenges facing her. She believed it was about getting the right strategy in place, which was correct, but she also needed to work on her inner game to see for herself what I and many others saw in her.

Her uncompromising attitude is what enabled her to eventually take the plunge to leave her corporate job and catapult her business to success.

She is now in high demand within her industry as a thought leader and speaker running 'The Mental Wealth Academy'.

If you want to take your inner game to the next level and start living the life that you want, you must have a zero tolerance attitude toward lowering your standards. This does not require anyone else to do anything. It requires you to become focused, structured and disciplined – the root of your freedom and success. People who are doing what they love and making things happen never compromise on their standards.

Of course, first you need to know what your standards are. What will you not tolerate? A good place to start is to understand your values, which we'll talk about more later.

This is a powerful exercise. When you live by what is important to you, it's easy to deal with challenges, spot opportunities, say no and focus on the things that empower and feed your soul. When you are clear on what your values are, look for how these manifest in your life and start to take actions based on them. When you do, things start to align and flow a bit easier.

For example, these are my values:

- Growth
- Simplicity
- Excellence
- Collaboration

How do these values manifest in and impact my life?

Growth: If I am not growing, my energy is low. In my work, I also I love helping others to grow. This value makes it easy for me to choose what I want to work on and who to surround myself with.

Simplicity: I find that we tend to overcomplicate things. Yes, detail is important, but it's easier to win when you keep things simple and manageable.

Excellence: I want to ensure there is excellence in the work I do for my clients and in how I show up in the world. This value keeps me on my toes and drives me to improve each day.

Collaboration: It's no fun doing everything on your own. Collaborating with like-minded people is fun, empowering and immensely satisfying when done well.

4. Get out of your own way

We all have opinions, but they can get in your way and be a barrier to your success, stopping you from reaching your potential and creating a bottleneck in your progress. I'm not saying the opinions you have are wrong – even a broken clock is right twice a day. I'm saying that many of your opinions will be based on assumptions and a particular view of the world that is not conducive to success.

Success leaves clues, as Tony Robbins says.[1] Where do you look for these clues? A good place to start is other successful people. There are certain mantras they tend to live by that lead them to success, such as:

- The more you fail, the more you succeed.
  You cannot be truly successful unless you are prepared to fail. You don't *have* to fail to succeed, but if you've never failed, it suggests you've not pushed yourself or gone beyond what you believed was possible.

- Your impossible is someone else's possible. The only difference is your mindset. A lot of the things I talk about in this book start with mindset.

- You don't and will never know it all. Get a team and a mentor. You haven't got all the answers – you haven't even always got the right questions. The people around you will play a huge role in your successful.

- There is more than one way to do anything. Your opinion may lead you down a particular path, which might get you what you want, but perhaps not in the most effective or efficient way. There is no right or wrong way, just alternative ways.

---

1   T Robbins (@tonyrobbins), 'Success leaves clues…' (25 July 2017), https://twitter.com/tonyrobbins/status/889864526719467520?lang=en-GB

- The 'how' will always change. You can plan and create a roadmap, but things change and numerous factors will determine what the next steps will be. You might want to know the ten steps to reach your A-game, but you may only know steps one and two initially, with step three being determined by the outcome of step two.

When you ask people what is in the way of their success, lack of resources and time are immediately cited. I'm not saying these aren't factors, but often we don't conduct an audit of how resourceful we are, working out what we can actually do with the resources we have; or a time audit, looking at whether we are using the time we have available to us in the most efficient way.

This comes back to your inner game. It's about being honest with yourself and squeezing whatever you can out of what you have. When you think only about your next step – not the whole roadmap, not the end goal, just the next step – and what's stopping you from taking it, if you are honest, it's probably you.

This may seem harsh. But think about it: is taking the next step possible, with the time and resources you have right now? I bet it is. Take that step, trust the process and see what you discover about yourself. This is the first level of your foundation – take whatever next step is possible in your current circumstances and get out of your own way.

5. No longer a victim

Now is not the time to be or play the victim. If this has been your mindset, change it and embrace the new you. If you want to play your A-game you cannot play the victim, no matter how unfair something might seem.

A person with a victim mentality:

- Feels sorry for themselves, disguises the truth, resists change and remains stuck in the same position

- Waits for someone or something to come and save them

- Has a false sense of entitlement

- Believes other people dictate their life so feels powerless and doesn't take any responsibility for their life

- Blames others for their feelings, results and the situation they find themselves in

- Feels that the world is against them

- Expects to gain sympathy from others and, when they don't get it, feels upset

The opposite of being a victim is taking ownership of your life. A person who takes ownership of their life:

- Knows that life happens for them just as it does for everyone else, and seeks to learn from every situation, good or bad

- Takes 100% responsibility for the way they feel and where they are in life

- Doesn't hide from the truth, is kind to themselves, makes changes and continues to make progress

- Finds solutions to problems they face and takes on their own power

- Is grateful for everything they have, however small

- Celebrates others' success

- Knows how to say no powerfully

The distinction is clear. Look, I get it, there are days when you think life is totally and utterly unfair, when whatever you do you don't get the results you want. What I suggest is, when life seems hard and nothing is happening for you, give yourself a pocket of time to feel sorry for yourself. This could be five minutes or five hours, a few days even. Allow yourself that time, but then get back into action.

I appreciate this is simplistic, and of course I'm not talking here about those dealing with mental health issues and struggling to get through each day. What I'm talking about is those situations where you can choose either to be a victim or take empowered action. Playing your A-game is about having the self-awareness to recognise when you are allowing yourself to be a victim of circumstances.

Now that your foundations are set, it's time to look for, create and embrace opportunities.

Opportunities

In this section I explain how you can identify and create opportunities when you have the right foundation in place.

This section is all about the mindset (inner game) and behaviours (outer game) you need to embrace to *maximise* the opportunities that come in your path, but in some cases, you can create out of nothing, just by embracing a different way of thinking and following up that with the right intentional actions.

6. Embrace opportunities

There is a perception that some people get lots of opportunities and others don't get any. The truth lies somewhere in between. It would be naïve to say that where you are born, your socioeconomic status and your culture, doesn't have a bearing on the opportunities you encounter. But we all get opportunities; the extent to which you embrace those opportunities comes down to your mindset:

- Are you sceptical or optimistic?

- Do you embrace or shy away from risk?

- Do you question whether things are right for you?

Embracing opportunities is also about embracing the potential for transformational change.

An opportunity can be anything from something landing in your lap, to saying yes to what you'd normally say no to, or simply a moment where you make a decision about your life. All these can mean a big change.

How do you embrace that opportunity and turn it into progress? You need faith, belief, self-belief and confidence. In my experience, if you surround yourself with the right people, you are more likely to maximise your opportunities. You don't have to wait for these opportunities to come to you – you can create your own.

Performance coach Tony Robbins says you can look at your resources – ie the money, talent, skills and tools you have – and decide what opportunities you can take on or create for yourself.[2] Or, you can look at how resourceful you can be in maximising what you have.

Some ideas for how you can embrace new opportunities:

- **Accept that opportunities mean change.** Changes to how you feel, how others see you and how you act. Lean into this and trust the process.

- **Be curious and ask questions.** Curiosity is key to learning and you can never ask too many questions. Not only will this help you understand more about your situation but it will enable you to develop relationships with those around you. Going through a change together is better than attempting it alone.

- **Find a new comfort zone.** Be prepared to develop new habits, fail and embrace the unknown – this is where the magic lies.

- **Expect it to be hard.** If it was easy to embrace new opportunities, we would be doing it all the time. It will be hard at some point, this is your opportunity to grow.

- **Focus on the future.** To play your A-game and take ownership of your life and business, focus on what your new future could be. Whether an

---

2   T Robbins (@tonyrobbins), 'It's not lack of resource…' (22 January 2018), https://twitter.com/tonyrobbins/status/955455778512605184?lang=en

opportunity has been presented to you or you have created it, you are now in control of what your future could be.

Don't let a scarcity mindset make you believe that the opportunities you want are not available to you. There is abundance in the world, but only if you have an abundance mindset.

7. Create opportunities

Some opportunities just fall into your lap, and only require you to recognise and embrace them. Other times, you need to be more proactive in bringing those opportunities to your door. Below are five tips that, if you keep them in mind, will help you to acquire an abundance mindset and create opportunities for yourself:

1. **Get into the habit of paying attention**: Look at what is happening around you, in real life and on social media, not just on the surface but the underlying trends and recurrent themes. Observant people are more aware and more likely to have new opportunities occur to them. Become more aware and you'll grow as a person and make yourself a resource to those you work with.

2. **Accept how powerful you are**: Knowing your power means understanding your impact. Everything you do has an impact – the way you

present yourself, how you talk to and respond to people, how you listen and your actions. This impact and energy, if positive, creates opportunities because people want to be around you.

3. **Believe that opportunities are everywhere**: Know your values and what you want, then look for ideas and trends that align with your interests and skills. Develop a habit of looking at everything to see how you might improve it. Then take ownership of your ideas.

4. **Accept help**: Don't be too proud to accept help. When you have a great idea, look for support. You cannot build amazing things on your own, you need a team of like-minded people who share your values and work ethic. Let people know how much you love what you do – people are impressed by those who love their work, and will want to help.

5. **Be decisive**: Decide you will say yes and don't hesitate. You know which opportunities fit your interests and skills and which don't, but get into the habit of taking opportunities as a way of growing and acquiring new skills. Be open about the fact that you are always watching and learning and people will feel secure in offering opportunities that grow with you.

All of these mental shifts are effective, but only if you follow them with action. Part Two of this book will explain how to do this.

CASE STUDY: JO AND ZOE

Jo and Zoe ran their own bookkeeping businesses and met at an event just before the Covid-19 pandemic. They got talking and saw an opportunity to help other bookkeepers run and grow their businesses.

During the pandemic they barely saw each other, but their vision was so strong and the opportunity too good to miss, and they started 'The 6-Figure Bookkeeper'. Using the power of social media they began to grow a loyal following of bookkeepers.

During the pandemic, the social audio platform Clubhouse began to make waves, which was where I connected with Jo and Zoe. It offered a unique opportunity to hear people talk about 'their thing', like you would on a radio station. They seized this opportunity, recognising it was perfectly aligned with their business.

I finally met Jo and Zoe in person and we started to work together, focusing on them building an abundance mindset, fine tuning their strategy and taking consistent actions to grow their business. This helped them pull off their biggest launch to date.

8. Trust unconditionally

Trust is a funny thing, and can be approached in a logical and/or emotional way. Some people's default is to trust someone from the start, until it is broken. From an emotional perspective, you are opening yourself up, making yourself vulnerable. For others, you need to earn their trust; they approach things logically, looking for evidence of trust having been earned or lost. I am the former; I trust people from the start. Some would consider this naïve, even dangerous, and say that I'm opening myself up to being taken advantage of. I trust people unconditionally from the outset because that is how I would like others to approach me. How can you expect unconditional trust from others, if you don't offer it yourself?

I encourage you to trust unconditionally. By this, I don't mean you should trust someone forever or under any circumstances. What I mean is, trust someone from the outset and don't attach any conditions to that trust. This kind of trust feels different for both parties. When you understand the feelings associated with trust you can see why this is such a useful tactic. Trust fosters agreement, relaxation, companionship, friendship, love and comfort. When playing your A-game, you need to be open to opportunities, to see what others don't and to do things that may not come naturally. If you can trust unconditionally, most people will approach and respond to you in a positive way.

As I've already mentioned, nothing great is achieved alone. You need a team, people around you who you can trust. This kind of trust can lead to:

- **Shared values**: When you extend trust to the people you work with, there is a value exchange. These shared values then reinforce that trust.

- **NATO (Not Attached To Outcome)**: When you do something for someone else don't expect anything back . . . ever. What happens is that we expect a response and this affects our decision making. A sense of generosity without obligation builds trusting relationships and enables us to focus on our own needs and the actions we must take to achieve these needs.

- **Show your vulnerability**: When you show your hand first, it will disarm others. If you work with people who share the same values, there is only a very small possibility that they will take advantage of that.

If you want people around you to trust you, ensure they know that your trust comes without conditions.

9. Live as an intentional being

When you start to play your A-game, you start to live the life of an intentional being. What does that mean? To explain, I'll tell you the story of when I left my corporate job in 2007.

When you work for a salary in the corporate world, you have a safety net. You have targets set for you, a team around you, commitments. In general, you know that as long as you do your job, you will get paid at the end of each month. This keeps you in action mode.

If you work for yourself, as I did when I left my job to start my own business, you are very much on your own. It's up to you when you work. Whether you make that phone call, write that report, do that research, is up to you.

When you have a salaried job, you have good and bad days. But even on the bad days, as long as you turn up and do enough, you won't suffer too much. You still get paid, and others are still contributing and might be having better days than you. When you work for yourself, if you have a bad day and are not as productive as normal, don't get enough done, don't reach your goals, can't get focused, there is no one else there to help you pick up the pieces. On the flip side, though, when you work for yourself, the momentum you can build when a series of good things happen or you have a run of great days, means you can be highly productive and get some amazing results.

What I found is that when I was intentional in my behaviour, my actions and my mindset, I became more productive. I had far fewer bad days. I talk in this book about the difference between a fixed mindset, a growth mindset, an evolve mindset and an intentional mindset. When you understand the subtle differences between these four mindsets, you start to understand how you can be in complete control of the way you think and act, to get the results you want. This is what I call an intentional way of being.

When you are being intentional, you are intent on thinking a certain way, intent on taking action toward achieving a result that you want. The great thing about having this mindset is that, even when you don't get what you want, it's easier to look at what you did and reassess your actions and not continue wasting days, weeks and months of your time going down a road to somewhere you don't want to go.

There's a misconception that action is all about the result. The result is of course important, but if you focus on the end result in your day-to-day behaviours, you will miss the opportunities around you. You don't need to keep reminding yourself of your end destination. That's your vision, your overall mission. Instead, focus on what you need to do today to take you one step closer to that end goal. That won't change, but the journey that you have mapped to get to your end destination, will likely change many times, in multiple ways and for various reasons, as you grow and progress forward.

There will be obstacles that you don't envisage. For example, when the Covid-19 pandemic began, all of a sudden the route to what I wanted to achieve in my business needed to change – the way I delivered my masterclasses, my coaching, readjusting my working practices, it all changed. My vision for what I wanted to create in the end hasn't changed and won't change, but the path there has. With an intentional way of being, it's easier to do switch paths, because you're taking control of what you need to do each day. Most of us will have had to take actions that we hadn't planned to because of the global pandemic. We had no choice; we had to change and adapt in order to survive.

One fantastic consequence of an intentional way of being is that you alleviate and/or reduce your anxiety and stress, because you feel more in control. Stress and anxiety often occur when you feel out of control or when things are happening to you that you have little or no control over. When you are being intentional in your actions, you are choosing to take control of each day, which means you do the things you want to do. When outside circumstances challenge you or put you off balance, you're in a much better frame of mind to react to that situation in a positive and helpful way.

This takes practice, it doesn't come naturally, especially if you're someone who is often in a reactive mode. Being intentional means you're more responsive, not reactive – responsive both to your internal indicators and to outside influences.

10. Stop complaining

When you up your game, be prepared for a complaint-free life – in other words, stop moaning. There is no room for complaining, as it achieves nothing. I'm not talking about bad customer service or faulty products. I'm talking about the kind of complaints that trip off the tongue day to day, comments that benefit nobody.

This is part of the foundations you need to play your A-game, because when you start to live a complaint-free life, it rewires your brain to look for opportunities, to see the upside, the positive and the benefits in even the worst situations.

We are all guilty of complaining sometimes, but we have different triggers. To recognise and try and avoid these triggers so that you can live a complaint-free life, it's helpful to identify the different types of complainer:

1. **The Everyday Complainer**: These people are chronic complainers; they complain all the time, about everything and anything. These are glass half empty people; they find things to complain about where others can't see an issue. They drain the people around them and they usually drain themselves. Their energy is usually low and they cannot see the good, the positive in anything.

2. **The Self-Seeking Complainer**: These are
   people who complain about things that bother
   them because they are looking for validation,
   reassurance and empathy. They want to know
   that other people agree with them so they're not
   required to change their point of view. What they
   are actually doing is gathering evidence that they
   are right, that other people think the same way
   they do, that there's no reason for them to change.
   As we know, change is uncomfortable and so
   often we resist it, even though we know it can be a
   positive thing that helps us to grow.

3. **The Passive Complainer**: These are people who
   complain in a way that gives the impression that
   everything is 'fine' while still letting you know
   that they're not happy about something. They try
   to give the impression that they are generally a
   positive person who sees the best in people and
   situations, but they also want to make sure that
   their complaint is heard. An example would be 'I
   have to work weekends – but it's fine, I like to be
   busy', or 'so and so might have more money than
   me, but it's okay, I enjoy my life'. It's a complaint,
   but with a caveat.

When you know what kind of complainer you tend to
be, you can spot your triggers and replace a complaint
with an opportunity. This is much more proactive. See
your complaint instead as an observation, and look
for an opportunity. Something negative might have

occurred – what can you do about it? For example, you might want to complain, 'I don't earn enough money', but instead think, 'I could ask for a pay rise', 'I could look for a new job' or 'I can start my own business'. Living a complaint-free life does not mean you deny or ignore any negativity; you observe and identify the issue, but you immediately go into solution mode. This is more entrepreneurial thinking, it's playing your A-game, constantly looking for opportunity.

You can live a complaint-free life. If you come across something that you're not happy about, don't immediately complain; identify the real issue, look for a solution and take action.

11. Play full-out

It's time to be serious and play full-out. No more off days. Off moments, maybe. Taking time out to reset, yes. But no unintentional off days. It won't work. Just be intentional. When you have good days, you ride the momentum; when you have bad days, you work through it. You can take time out and fill up your tank. If you are intentional about this you can take time out without guilt. When you need help, reach out. When you are being productive, stay on that path.

Play full-out to create the life you deserve, play full-out in your intentions, and play full-out in your manner of being. You have one life. One big opportunity.

Don't waste it. Adopt the tactics, strategies and concepts in this book, and you will start to live the life you desire. It won't be easy. You need to choose to play full-out every single day. Otherwise, you may as well be playing with one hand behind your back.

Play full-out, mind, body and spirit, and I promise you will start to create miracles in your life.

12. Start a conversation

Words change the world, and conversations can change your life. In my experience, most problems can be solved with a conversation. Chit chat is easy, but we often avoid critical, courageous, intentional conversations. By nature, we don't like conflict, so we shy away from the difficult conversations that we don't really want to have, because we fear it may lead to conflict or rejection that we don't feel resilient enough to deal with.

When you have an intentional conversation, three things can occur:

1. You get what you expect or what you want from the conversation

2. You don't get what you expect, or you get something that you don't want

3. A miracle happens

I want to focus on the third possibility from an intentional conversation: a miracle. In this context, a miracle is something unexpected, but welcome. Something that would not, could not, have occurred without that conversation taking place. Playing your A-game means having lots of conversations. This means you need to be brave, pick up the phone, go to events, approach people, ask for introductions and don't be too fixated on the outcome. Do this with the intention simply of having the conversation and see what you can create.

CASE STUDY: KPMG

I worked with thirty directors to improve leadership skills and communication. The core of the work I did was to encourage the directors to start conversations with an intention to really listen and understand what their teams needed in order to be more productive, and then commit to creating the environment necessary for them to enable that.

I encouraged an increased focus on the skill sets of the individual team members and leading the teams from a place of inspiring them to be their best.

We received excellent feedback on the hugely effective leadership transformation and communication skills following the Freedom Formula, and by simply starting conversations.

---

13. Live a non-negotiable life

I suggest that you aim to live a non-negotiable life. But what does that mean? Negotiation is about stating your position, acknowledging someone else's position and then trying to find some middle ground, a compromise. Living a non-negotiable life means a life without compromise, lived entirely on your terms, your values.

This book is about how to play *your* game. Not anyone else's, not the game of people you admire or respect. It's your game, your life, so you should be playing by your rules. This is not about anarchy, being contrary, going against the grain, causing disruption for the sake of it. It's about being true to yourself and your values.

When you live by your values, life becomes easier. If you have compromised on your values, the journey to adapting and re-aligning your life will be harder, but it can still be done quickly.

As I mentioned at the start of this book, in January 2019 I committed to losing weight and getting fitter. I was compromising on my values of being healthy and being an example to others through my lifestyle. To live according to my values, with the help of a fitness and health coach I identified some non-negotiable practices and habits. Healthier eating habits were now non-negotiable. Not missing a gym session became non-negotiable. Being tee-total became non-negotiable. I didn't focus on what I needed to do, but on what I wanted in my life and collaborated with an expert to put an appropriate plan in place to get there.

When you want to play your A-game you have to ask yourself: what is non-negotiable for me? What are the things you cannot negotiate on in order to have the life you want? This might be:

- Who you listen to

- Who and what you say yes to

- What you are not prepared to do

- The people you associate with

- How you want to spend your time

- What you might have previously given up
  because of circumstances or mindset

Reading this book, you decided that you want to play a bigger game, and especially your A-game. This is the start of your non-negotiable life and becoming who you want to be. In *Change Your Game*, I talk about owning your space – this is being non-negotiable. You decide who you want to become and then you set out your stall.

Make a list of the things that are non-negotiable in your life and then think about what mindset you need to adopt, what actions you need to take and what strategy you need to employ to ensure you do not compromise on these things. If you do that, your life will never look the same again.

14. Allow yourself to be unstuck

You might not think that you're stuck. The fact that you are reading this book and wanting to play your A-game means you likely feel stuck in some part of your life and/or business. There is a massive difference between saying that you want more and want to be unstuck and actually doing what it takes to get there. You have to believe that everything that you want is possible for you and within your grasp. It might not be immediately within your grasp, but it's possible.

First, you have to be prepared to consider things you've never contemplated before, to consider that perhaps the way you have been running your life and your business is not the most effective way. This will open up many new possibilities. Be sceptical, but don't be cynical. Be cautious, but not over cautious. Take risks, but calculated ones. This open-mindedness, allowing yourself to become unstuck, will feel like freedom, like there's a weight off your shoulders. You are telling yourself there is no pressure. You don't have to perform, you don't have to get a result, all you need to do is to reflect and be open to possibilities.

Then, anything is possible. This is how you allow yourself to become unstuck.

15. The Be Do Have model

You can use the Be Do Have model to get yourself unstuck.[3] This was a game changer for me. Most people live from right to left – they start with what they want, then think about what they do and finally who they want to be.

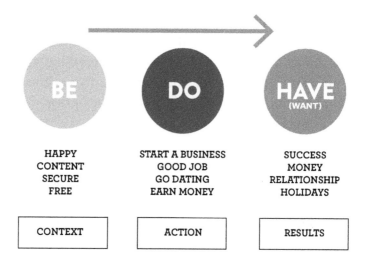

HAPPY	START A BUSINESS	SUCCESS
CONTENT	GOOD JOB	MONEY
SECURE	GO DATING	RELATIONSHIP
FREE	EARN MONEY	HOLIDAYS

CONTEXT	ACTION	RESULTS

The context from which you are operating

---

3 S Covey, *The 7 Habits of Highly Effective People* (Simon & Schuster, 2017)

Growing up in life, we are constantly asking ourselves what we want. We want more money. We want the perfect partner. We want an amazing house, fantastic holidays. We want a successful business or a high-flying career. We want to be surrounded by nice things. It's not just us. Society, our parents, family and friends are constantly asking us, what do we want?

Once we've thought about what we want first and foremost, our mind naturally goes next to what we need to do to get it. For example, if I want to be a doctor, what I need to do is get a medical degree. If I want to find a partner, I need to go dating. If I want lots of money, I need to start a profitable business or get a high-salary job.

Immediately, you are starting from a premise of what you want and then deciding what you need to do. You might think that there is nothing wrong with that. The problem is that there isn't one formula for life that can get you everything you want.

For example, say you want to run a successful tech company. Say, conveniently, that Steve Jobs or Bill Gates has created a manual, telling you exactly how they did it. If you follow their formula to the letter, are you guaranteed the success they had? Obviously, the answer is no. You might do well, but it's unlikely you will replicate their journey.

Even so, in the information era and age of the internet, we have so much information at our fingertips and are always being told how to do X, Y and Z. If it were just about the things you need to do, and information was all you needed to get the life you want, we'd all be living our dreams. It doesn't work like that.

Look at the Be Do Have model – most people live from right to left: what do I want? What do I need to do, so I can get what I want? Who they end up being is a product of that.

Now flip the model and look at it from left to right. Instead of starting with what you want to have, start with who you want to be – what kind of impact you want to have on the world, what kind of person you want to be, what kind of purpose you want to fulfil.

What you want to have is still important, but whatever it is (financial freedom, a partner, happiness and contentment, a legacy), consider who you need to *be* to get those things. From there, next think about what you need to do to become that person. Then, every single day, every single moment, focus on who you want to be and what that person needs to do. The result, what you have, will then look after itself.

What's interesting is that the things that you do, whether you come from a position of what you want to have, or from a position of who you want to be, are often more or less the same, but the energy is completely different. When you are thinking about what you want to have, you are attached to the outcome; if you then don't get it, you can become demotivated. When you are thinking about who you want to be, even if you don't get the result you want, it's not a failure; you can continue being who you need to be and maybe change or adapt your actions. You're not attached to the outcome. With this energy driving your actions, the opportunities for success are greater. You're better equipped to deal with 'failure' as you're no longer under pressure to be anybody but who you choose to be.

This takes courage. This takes intentional thinking and a strategic approach to life where you decide who you want to be and what that person needs to do. This is the premise that underlies everything I do in my world: how I develop my business, how I serve my clients, how I make an impact on the world. Ask yourself: who do I need to be to create the life I want?

The Resistance

In this section, we will address the feelings and thoughts that occur when we have breakthroughs and breakdowns in business and life. What to look out for, how to respond (and not react) and ways to cope with the reality of life.

16. Self-awareness

We are all born as blank slates; as we mature, we acquire 'stuff'. This stuff is the world through the eyes of other people, the reality that we are exposed to, how we deal with things we don't like or don't want and how we react to different situations.

Incidentally, you are not what you think you are. As Charles Cooley, an American sociologist said, 'I am not who you think I am, I am not who I think I am, I am who I think you think I am.'[4] Without a level of self-awareness, you will go on living in the world according to who you think others think you are. In this context, the resistance you feel when considering a change can come from emotions and feelings arising at multiple levels.

You now have the foundation in place to play your game, but when you start actually playing, you are going to encounter massive resistance. You are changing your reality; this is a big thing and you need to know how to *respond* not *react* to the resistance you will feel.

You have to accept what is real, whether you want it to be or not, and acknowledge the good, the bad and the ugly. If you don't, you are fighting a losing battle. This can be confronting because you might not like, or even hate, what you see, which is painful.

Without that self-reflection and self-awareness, you won't be able to get there. Facing this, your mind will resist. Your inner critic, or what the Buddhists call your monkey mind, will kick in. The monkey mind never stays still; it is restless, unsettling, confusing, indecisive and uncontrollable. This part of the brain

4   C Cooley, *Human Nature and the Social Order* (Charles Scribner's Sons, 1902)

is connected to the ego, which is constantly telling you, 'You are not good enough, you can't do anything right', which stops you from growing and moving forward. It is futile trying to ignore the monkey mind, you have to learn to tame it. We will learn how to do that in this chapter.

Your A-game will come to fruition when you start to respond to life and not react. When you react, you are driven by emotion, with little logic; when you respond, you are driven by logic, though acknowledging emotion. When you acknowledge and control your emotions you make better decisions, which lead you to the life you want. The more you practise this, the better you will get at it, but it won't happen overnight. You will fail some days and that's okay. Recognise these moments, when the monkey mind gets louder, and use the techniques outlined in this part of the book to tame it.

17. Responding to resistance

When we talk about resistance, the only place to start is your mind. This is where your biggest resistance will be.

Your mind will resist. More specifically, the reptilian part of your mind, your survival instinct, will resist. It doesn't want to take risk. It doesn't want you to expose yourself to possible harm. It wants to protect you. It's not creative. It's not progressive. It's not entrepreneurial.

How do you respond to resistance? In three ways:

1. **Go back to your why**: Your bigger reason; your vision; your purpose; your values. What do you want to create? Every time you feel resistance, go back to this – the business you want to create, the impact you want to have.

2. **Allow the resistance**: Acknowledge the resistance and allow it to be there. Don't try and fight it, just think about why it's cropped up. It could be that you're just not feeling great that day, or it could be related to your self-worth, or perhaps your abilities. Just sit with it. Don't get emotionally attached to the resistance and make up stories about why it is there. Just sit with it and accept it. Then allow it to dilute and dissipate.

3. **Learn and evolve**: Do what you're doing now – read books that educate, surround yourself with people who inspire, speak to a mentor, lean into the learning process.

You are not alone in this. All resistance starts with the mind. How you deal with it will depend on the work that you do. The 'work' here is self-development work, it's the work you do on yourself. The traditional school system in western society does not encourage this work. We are left to our own devices to try and be the best human we can be. Mental health and self-awareness are typically only addressed from the perspective of repair or cure, not prevention and wellbeing.

There are some great titles that can help you with doing the work in this field, such as *Think and Grow Rich* by Napoleon Hill,[5] *The 7 Habits of Highly Effective People* by Stephen Covey[6] and *The Magic of Thinking Big* by David Schwartz.[7] These are just three among many books that talk about the work we need to do as humans to be the best version of ourselves.

18. Time is never an excuse

One of the common excuses that we all make for ourselves is lack of time (the other one is money). Now that you have decided to play your A-game, you can never, ever use time as an excuse again. Consider this. When you say you're 'busy', what you're really saying is, 'I'm doing lots of things, I have no spare time, so I must be successful.' This doesn't necessarily mean you're doing the things that you want to do, or the things that make you most productive.

---

5   N Hill, *Think and Grow Rich* (Chump Change, 1937)
6   S Covey, *The 7 Habits of Highly Effective People* (Simon & Schuster, 2017)
7   D Schwartz, *The Magic of Thinking Big* (Vermilion, 2016)

Instead of being busy, you want to be productive and effective. I made a commitment to myself that I will never be busy again. If you look at my days, they are packed full with things I need to do – meetings, creating content, making sales, coaching, training. But whatever I'm doing, I'm just doing that one thing. When I finish, I move on to the next thing. I don't allow myself to multitask, to focus simultaneously on all the things I have to do in my life and get overwhelmed with feeling 'busy'. What does busy look, feel and sound like? It's chaotic, overwhelming and noisy.

The impact that refusing to be busy has on my life is that I am more productive, have more energy and get things finished. Despite never being busy, I'm always occupied. I do lots of things. I do what I intend to do; I aim to be as productive and efficient as possible. Do I always succeed? Of course not. I'm human. My intention is that I don't want to be busy, but I do want to be effective. It's about reframing your time and how you spend it.

Another aspect of time management is lateness. I intend never to be late for anything. How can you make that commitment? When you go about your day, various things will be outside of your control that could make you late – delayed trains, missed buses, traffic. I get it.

I start with the intention that I will not be late. This is about how I turn up in my head and approach my life. The focus should be on preparation and the structure that needs to be in place, forcing your behaviour to change.

I tell all my clients, 'I will never be late for a session.' As a result of making this commitment, I will organise my day in such a way that guarantees I will be on time. I never try and squeeze a call in; I say no to other opportunities; and I manage the expectations of other people and projects to ensure that I am always on time. What that does, which is especially important in the work that I do, is show the client that your words, actions and behaviour have influence and impact. When you align the influence of your words and actions, you become unbeatable.

Ask yourself what changes you need to make in your business and your life to ensure that you are never late for meetings, you deliver projects on time, you call when you say you will. It's satisfying and extremely liberating when you make that commitment.

Highly successful people have exactly the same amount of time that you do. What's different is that they are resourceful with that time. They maximise their opportunities, which also means resting and doing things that take your mind off the job. Your brain cannot be creative twenty-four seven. It's up to you to create pockets of time that allow you to be highly productive. This also means ensuring you take time out to get good rest, which I talk more about in

Change Your Game. Take a moment to think about what your life would be like if you made this commitment, how much would change for the better.

19. You're stuck

You are either stuck, or you're not. What determines this is your mindset. People commonly believe that they are stuck because of:

- Lack of ideas

- Lack of money

- Lack of contacts

- Lack of resources

- Lack of opportunities

- Not knowing where to start

- Believing they are not ready

These are common misconceptions. Maybe right now some of the above are holding you back, but when you let go in your mind of feeling stuck, opportunities start to open up. This book will help get you unstuck.

In *Change Your Game*, I said, 'I am interested in your excuses in as much as I can dismantle them to show you what is possible.' Excuses are just that, excuses; reason gives you an opportunity to become unstuck. You can only play your A-game when you are unstuck.

As you work through this book and absorb the strategies and concepts, keep in mind that:

- You can achieve anything you want with the right mindset and strategy.

- Action, however small, will always produce a result.

- Who you surround yourself with will have a massive impact on your productivity.

- Knowing is not enough, you must implement what you know.

Whatever your current circumstances, if you free yourself to play your game and implement the recommendations in this book, your life will become unrecognisable.

Becoming unstuck is not complicated. I have a very simple philosophy for life: simplicity is the route to all success. Of course, not everything is simple, some things are naturally complex. What I mean is that you shouldn't overcomplicate things.

I have already talked in this book about being stuck and how to get unstuck. I don't know what your background is, what you've been through, what your dreams are. But what I do know is that you want to change, you want to play a different game – your game.

Everything I talk about in this book will help you to get unstuck, once you recognise that you are stuck. You have to be patient and trust the process, but the approach you need to take in your life to play your A-game is not complicated. Anybody, with any background, any dreams, can make this kind of progress.

In my CYG model, there are three determinants of success: your mindset, which is the context of your life and your impact; the roadmap you create for yourself, ie your strategy or game plan; and finally the outer game, which is your actions, because without taking action, nothing can happen. Each of these is simple to understand.

This book gives you a manual and a set of resources that you can apply to your life, regardless of talent or skill. It's about intent. It's about creating intent in your life and in your actions, and it's about believing in the results. It's also about accepting failure, that it's okay to fail because it's always a lesson and can help you move forward.

Allow yourself to be unstuck and don't overcomplicate the process.

20. Bold mindset versus growth mindset

The growth mindset is a simple idea introduced by world-renowned Stanford University psychologist Carol Dweck.[8] It describes a mindset that is open to learning and trying new ideas, that embraces challenge and takes on feedback. It is the polar opposite of a fixed mindset, which gives up easily, sticks to what it knows, doesn't like a challenge and avoids failure at all costs. A growth mindset is essential if you are to have any success, and developing this mindset should be a core focus of all education.

What's the difference between a growth mindset and a bold mindset? Both are important and valuable, but a bold mindset is at another level. A bold mindset is one that sets big goals that are visionary and aligned with your values.

People with a bold mindset have certain key characteristics:

- They know their worth.
- It's not 'if' but 'when'.
- It's never about them, it's always about the bigger picture.
- They want to help others succeed.
- They are game changers.
- They won't accept no for an answer.
- They see a world of abundance.

8   C Dweck, *Mindset: The new psychology of success* (Ballantine Books, 2007)

- It's never just about money.

- They practise legacy thinking.

- They accept change.

It is this last one that can be the deal breaker. We live in a time when we have a huge amount of information published on the internet every minute. Research shows that the average American consumes about 34 gigabytes of information each day, an increase of about 350% compared to thirty years ago.[9] This information includes new ideas, concepts, perspectives, opportunities and the thing that is the most often resisted but that has to be adopted by those with bold mindsets – technology.

Technological advances affect how we grow a business, develop products, find jobs, build networks, advertise, communicate. Yet the resistance to technological change is tangible. This resistance is futile. Four areas where the advancement of tech will affect all of our lives, whatever your opinion is, are:

- Blockchain

- Driverless cars

- Augmented reality

- Artificial intelligence

9   N Bilton, 'Part of the Daily American Diet, 34 Gigabytes of Data', *New York Times*, 2009, www.nytimes.com/2009/12/10/technology/10data.html

Without bold mindsets, technology would not be part of our lives. If you don't adopt a bold mindset yourself, you will be one of the late adapters and among the last to benefit.

I am assuming that, as you are reading or listening to this book, you don't have a fixed mindset. But playing your A-game requires you to have a bold mindset, not just a growth mindset. There is nothing wrong with a growth mindset; most of what you want to do can be achieved with this mindset. But having a bold mindset can take you to a place you could not even have contemplated before.

21. Take off your pink-tinted glasses

Whatever stage of life you're at, you will have your pink-tinted glasses. This is how you see the world, your perception, your truth. When it comes to making changes in your life and looking to achieve new things, you have to adopt a different mindset. Playing your A-game pushes your standards higher, for which you need to take those glasses off and see the world differently, to see it how it actually is.

How is it that you come to be wearing these pink-tinted glasses that give you a one-dimensional view of the world? Imagine you are eight years old and you meet me, I am an authority figure, someone you respect and listen to. I point to a big, lush tree next to us and ask you what colour it is. You say green. Then I tell you to put some pink-lensed glasses on and ask you, 'What colour is the tree now?' This time, you say, 'It looks pink but really it's green,' because you know that the glasses you just put on have changed your perspective.

Then I tell you that from now on, you have to wear those glasses twenty-four seven and if you ever take them off, something bad is going to happen. Remember I'm an authority figure and you are eight years old – the odds are, you're going to do what I say.

I see you a week later and ask you again what colour the tree is. At this point, you likely remember me and our conversation and you tell me that the tree looks pink but you know that the colour is green and it's the glasses that make it look pink. I remind you that you cannot ever take those glasses off and if you do, something bad is going to happen.

As time goes by, you start to forget you have the glasses on and go about your life seeing the world through this filter that you've become oblivious to. Thirty years later we meet again. Can you remember a conversation you had thirty years ago? What about ten or fifteen years ago? It's unlikely. I ask you again what colour the tree is. You say it's pink, I tell you it's green. You have been wearing the glasses for thirty years, everything looks pink, but you don't know that anymore. When I say the tree is green, you're going to be convinced that it's pink. The reality is, the tree is green. But in *your* reality, the tree is pink. In order for you to see my reality, which happens to be the true reality, you have to take the pink-tinted glasses off.

The pink-tinted glasses represent your opinions, fears, observations, perspectives and your potentially narrow reality. We all live in our own reality. Those who are brave enough to take their glasses off have the opportunity to see a different reality, which can open up all sorts of new opportunities and perspectives.

Playing your A-game means taking the pink-tinted glasses off and looking at the world differently. Your opinions can hold you back and sometimes your perspective will be your greatest barrier. Now you know that you're wearing them, you have a choice: you can either keep the glasses on, stay safe, I'm fine with what I need to achieve; or you can take the chance to glimpse a different world, put your opinions and perspective to one side, have different conversations and create different opportunities.

The Reality

In this section, we are going to talk about the reality of what is happening in your life and what you're trying to do, the things that you need to be aware of in order to make bold, empowered choices.

22. Keep momentum

Playing your A-game does not mean you are superhuman and it does make you fallible. The key is to understand yourself, be kind to yourself, but always remain conscious and keep momentum.

We have this perception that highly successful people must have some secret sauce, or they had a lucky break, or were given more opportunities than the rest of us. These may or may not be true. The one thing that I have seen that is consistent among people who play their A-game is that they create and maintain momentum.

In physics, momentum is defined as mass in motion. All objects have a mass and if an object is moving, then it has momentum – in other words, mass in motion. The momentum is affected by two variables, how much of the stuff is moving (its size/weight) and how fast it's moving. Let's apply this law in the context of entrepreneurship.

The 'stuff' or 'object' in this context will be a project you're working on, your business or a part of your life. The variables impacting on its momentum are how big or important that work is to you and how fast you're working on it. If it's a big piece of work that you're really passionate about, your greater motivation will mean you work faster on it, which will create greater momentum.

It is easier to push a moving object than a stationary one. Using micro goals, breaking down bigger goals into smaller parts and making sure you win every day, will help you to create and maintain momentum. I will be talking about micro goals in more detail later in this book.

In sport, we often hear the term used. A team that has momentum is on the move. Once they have a couple of wins under their belt, they likely to have more, because they've got momentum. The same is true in life and in business. If you leave too big a gap between actions, you'll miss out on the maximising impact of the momentum created by the first action. This momentum is key to great success while playing your A-game – taking small, regular actions all the time creates a momentum that will increase their impact.

23. Breakdown

Any journey to achieve a personal, business or sporting success will inevitably face barriers. A point of breakdown is common, when you fall apart and feel you can no longer go on, that there's no way forward. It's a predictable moment.

Once you understand that breakdowns are predictable and are followed by breakthroughs, it's much easier to navigate the journey to the success you're looking for, especially in the entrepreneurial space. In 1949 Joseph Campbell outlined what he called the hero's journey, which he said always followed a predictable pattern, regardless of the character or genre.[10] The 'hero' of the story always faces conflict and meets challenges and ultimately triumphs through adversity. The journey, according to Campbell, comprises three acts. In the

10   J Campbell, *The Hero with a Thousand Faces* (MJF Books, 1949)

first act, the hero leaves the comfort and familiarity of their own world and enters a new one. The second act is spent in this unknown territory where our hero is confronted with challenges, obstacles and negativity. In the third act, they return triumphant.

The process of growing a business, changing your life, or trying to achieve your dreams follows the same pattern, which can be further broken down into twelve stages.

In stage one you are in the ordinary world, the world as you see it now. It's predictable, familiar and you understand it. It's also frustrating because in this ordinary world you can't achieve what you want to. Then you enter stage two, you have this calling, this need to do something different, to design a new life or business, to seize an opportunity. It is the call to adventure, to go and make things happen.

But this call to adventure requires you to confront what you want and push yourself outside your comfort zone. It challenges your thought processes and makes you consider what is possible. It forces you to confront the challenge now you need to rise to, but you're only human and the first time you are called to change, you resist, you come up with excuses. 'What if I'm not good enough? What if it's not for me? It's the wrong time.' You refuse the call. This is stage three.

While you're in this state of mind, all that is going through your mind is that this is not the right time for you. The key to overcoming this fear is the mentor who you meet in stage four. This mentor can take many forms. It might be an individual, a trusted family member, a group of like-minded people. It could be someone who you admire from afar who inspires you to make a change, because you can relate to their story.

If the mentor is someone you know and can speak with, their support will be much more impactful. They will hold you accountable, help to overcome your initial fears, push you to achieve your dreams, ensure you are committed to the change and empower you to take the first step across the threshold into stage five, toward change.

Then, in stage six, you begin to test the boundaries of this new world. Here you realise who your true allies and enemies are, who will support you in your new intentional way of being. You start to break conventional rules, start to question if this new world is for you. Can you handle this change? Are you prepared for what this new world means for you, in all areas of your life?

At stage seven you face a massive test. You are preparing for major change and now you have to confront your innermost fears. Am I really that person I want to be? Internal conflict arises, making you resistant and preventing you from making the change. But it's too late now, you've committed, you're going to go for it, you're there.

At stage eight you are at the point of a re-birth, following the death of the old you. All of the new habits you have developed through stages five, six and seven mean that at stage eight you don't recognise how you were operating before. This can be tough. You might start to wonder why you didn't make this change before, why you waited so long. Remember, everything happens when it is supposed to. The most important thing in this stage is to lean into and trust the process.

The length of time you spend in each stage depends on you: the change you are making, how willing you are to fail fast, how much you want it and your individual circumstances. The journey can be short or long, but what is predictable is the stages you must move through. Getting through stage eight means you get to experience the reward. You start seeing the fruits of the seeds you have sown. This reward is the external validation you are looking for. Nevertheless, throughout the journey, your internal feelings and courage is what you need to trust.

You now accept this new way of life. You think, 'Wow, I like this new person', and there's no going back. You're the hero. Now at stage ten, you return to your old world, with your new way of being, and say, 'Look, this is the new me.'

Often, when you go back to your new world, there's a final test. Stage eleven is the reaction of those who know the old you. Are you strong enough to continue to be the new you? Some people in your old world might not understand the new you. Others look at you and be inspired to change too; or they might be threatened by you and the change you've made.

Finally, you reach the final step, stage twelve, where you master this new intentional way of being. You've returned and been tested, held strong, and you know for sure that you are the new you.

The hero's journey is predictable. Once you're on that journey, you need to keep taking the next step, then the next. Each stage will bring new villains, new challenges, but as the hero, you will deal with these moments in a predictable way. Looking at the diagram, what point in the hero's journey are you at now? Identify this and you'll know what's coming next. This is where you need to be.

It's a powerful archetype, a powerful image to hold onto. When you're going through tough times, it will help you to know that there is light at the end of the tunnel. As an exercise, identify where you're at in your hero's journey right now, based on what challenges you are currently facing in your life. Then you can identify who you need to be and what you need to do to reach the next stage of your journey.

24. Imposter syndrome

Before I tackle how to overcome imposter syndrome, we need to define exactly what it is:

> Imposter syndrome refers to an internal experience of believing that you are not as competent as others perceive you to be. While this definition is usually narrowly applied to intelligence and achievement, it has links to perfectionism and social context.[11]

---

11 A Cuncic, 'What Is Imposter Syndrome?', VeryWell Mind, 2022, www.verywellmind.com/imposter-syndrome-and-social-anxiety-disorder-4156469

In my opinion, it's not a syndrome, but a set of symptoms. You suffer from a feeling that you don't belong, you don't know enough, like others are ahead of you. A feeling of self-doubt. A feeling that you will get 'found out' or discovered as a fake. You have an inability to assess your true skills, talent and competences. You attribute any success you may have to either luck or external factors. You sabotage your own success.

The truth is, none of these assumptions and beliefs are true and you should not make any decisions based on them. Yet in some instances, 'imposter syndrome' can actually improve performance, depending on the type of symptoms you experience. It can manifest in different ways for different people.

The Expert: Experts are always trying to learn more and are never satisfied with their level of understanding. This leads them to underestimate their abilities even though they are often highly skilled. If this is you, recognise your skills for what they are and focus on who can benefit from your wisdom. Don't get consumed by your need to know more and fall into a cycle where, the more you discover, the more you realise you still don't know.

The Creative: Creatives set lofty goals for themselves and then feel crushed when they don't succeed on their first try. If this is you, set big but realistic goals but then detach yourself from the outcome and focus on the process. Recognise the small achievements and learn from the failures on the way.

The Perfectionist: Perfectionists are never satisfied and always strive to do their best. Rather than focusing on their strengths, they tend to dwell on faults or mistakes, often leading to a high degree of stress and anxiety. If this is you, be aware of your need for perfection but focus on just the next step, not on making the whole picture perfect. Your willingness to set and desire to reach high standards is a positive thing. But remember that perfection doesn't exist. You will never get there. Accept what is.

The Individualist: Individualists have a strong sense of self-worth that they link closely to their productivity, so they tend not to accept offers of assistance. Asking for help is often seen as a sign of weakness or incompetence. Stubbornness and a desire to stay in your own lane, when harnessed in the right way, can lead to great success. But if this is you, remember that no one has ever achieved anything great on their own; behind every success is always a team.

The Superhero: Superheroes feel inadequate and this motivates them to work hard. There is nothing wrong with a hard-working attitude but you should practise gratitude and recognise the small achievements too. Remember you can still be brave, vulnerable and show your weakness.

What's ironic is that if you have these feelings, it means you already have some evidence of success. A true imposter would not have these feelings. When they arise, use it as a moment of gratitude, a moment to recognise what you have achieved rather than comparing yourself to others who are in different chapters of their life.

25. Freedom Formula

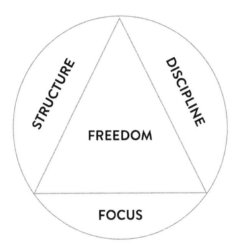

Freedom is a tricky thing to navigate. We all want it, but we're not always willing to do what we need to do to get it. Freedom also means different things to different people; you need to work out the discipline and the freedom you want and whether you're doing the right things to get there. To understand what freedom means for you and where you currently are in your journey to reaching it, ask yourself some questions around the core components of the Freedom Formula – focus, discipline and structure:

Focus:

- What are you focusing on now?

- Do you have clarity on what you need to achieve?

- Do the actions you take each day align with where you want your focus to be?

Structure:

- Is your day structured in a way that maximises your output?

- Are you using tools and automation to optimise your efficiency?

- Does your structure allow you to overcome procrastination, overwhelm and overthinking?

Discipline:

- In what areas of your life do you need to improve your self-control?

- Are you clear about what success looks like at the end of each day?

- What level of accountability do you need to improve your discipline?

In my experience, when you can answer yes to those questions you will be able to create the freedom you desire. There is no magic pill, no secret sauce. No one is coming to save you. It's up to you. Life happens. Some of the cards we are dealt mean that freedom is so far away that we can't even imagine it. I am taking a punt here. You are reading this for a reason. You want it, you are prepared to go for it, even if you might be scared.

The Response

Once you are playing your A-game, are facing your new reality and have become aware of the natural resistance that occurs, you want to respond, not react. When you react you are led by emotion; when you respond you are calm and in control. You take full responsibility for your actions and understand that life doesn't happen *to* you, but *for* you. You respond in a way that enables you to grow, even in the most challenging times.

26. Lean in

Responding requires you to *lean in*. Typically, when confronted with an obstacle or a challenge, we tend to lean away, to defend, to retreat. But retreating from a challenge gets us nowhere. It is not conducive to growth or to playing your A-game. This was true even for prehistoric man. Cavemen would go out hunting and when they came across an animal that might attack them they might initially retreat, but they would soon realise that if they stayed away they would go hungry. To survive, they would have to lean into the challenge.

It's no different today. If you look at the people who truly play their A-game, they are always leaning into problems or challenges; they don't shirk their responsibilities or shy away from difficulty. They don't back away, they confront things head on. They might take a moment to assess the situation and the context, but they don't overthink it and they lean in.

To play your A-game, to understand how to get the results you want, you have to change your mindset from trying to avoid obstacles and challenges to embracing them.

There are five ways in which you can lean in:

1. **Accept the challenge.** Accept the situation and what's happening, and accept that you have to do something.

2. **Take a micro action.** That means doing something now, not putting it off. It could be that you call someone, you do some research, or you do *something* because the psychological impact of

having started something is that you feel good, which will increase your momentum.

3. **Be accountable.** Tell someone what you're doing, whether that's a mentor or group of individuals. Leaning in can be making a public declaration that you're doing this. I'm not saying you have to tell the world, but give yourself the gift of support from others.

4. **Keep checking in with yourself.** Are you on the right path? Does it feel right? If it doesn't, reach out to someone who you can talk things through with. When you lean into something you've got to keep checking in, to ensure you're not leaning into a situation that doesn't serve you.

5. **Have faith.** Don't be a perfectionist; you don't have to have everything perfect before you lean in. Leaning in means doing something even when everything isn't perfect, when you haven't got all the answers, you're not totally ready. Taking some action, even an imperfect action, will show how far you've come and that you don't need to do everything perfectly to get results.

27. NATO: Not attached to outcome

When I set out the Be Do Have model earlier in this book I explained how when you base your actions on who you want to Be rather than what you want to Have, the outcomes look after themselves. There is immense power to be gained from detaching from the outcome of your actions. This is because when you are emotionally attached to a desired outcome, in business or in life, there is an emotional charge. When you attach yourself to an outcome, you're relying on it working out. If it does, great, happy days, you celebrate and move on. If it doesn't work out and you're emotionally attached to what you thought the outcome was going to be, you're disappointed, distracted, drained. Imagine you're about to go into a meeting and are waiting for confirmation of a partnership, a sale or an opportunity. You're convinced it's in the bag and you've already started planning for it. Then you get a call and to your surprise they say no, it's not happening. Because you're so emotionally attached to that outcome, you're completely thrown off, your energy dips and it affects everything you do that day.

This is not to say that you shouldn't care about the consequences of your actions, that you shouldn't be disappointed, upset or even angry in some circumstances if something that you expect to happen doesn't, but you need to detach from the possible or expected outcome and trust the process so that you can focus on the task at hand. Have an outcome in mind, by all means, but once you've identified it, don't focus on it.

Think about a football match. All the players know that what they want and need to do is score more goals than the opposition. This is the only outcome that matters. But what they focus on is how they turn up, their strategies, teamwork and executing on the task at hand. They don't have to focus on the outcome they want, this is a given, they focus on the execution. As they are executing, they may need to adjust their strategies depending on micro outcomes, but they are not measuring their current progress against the ultimate outcome they want.

These expectations can prevent us from performing at our best. When we are attached to an outcome, we are not present and focused on the task at hand, so we are not giving ourselves the best chance to achieve our desired outcome. Of course, you want to know what you are aiming for, but when performing a task, you need to be completely present and 100% focused on maximising your performance. You cannot do this if your mind is on the outcome. Practise like it matters and perform like it doesn't. Having no expectations and not being afraid to make mistakes takes the pressure off. If you think that you only have one chance at success, you'll be scared of making a mistake, stressed in your body and mind, which will impact your performance.

It's easy to see and understand this in a sporting context, where the lines between competing and training are distinct. You know when it's competition time and when it's not. But how does this apply to life, work and business, when it's a constant struggle to be at your best all the time?

Because you're constantly performing, being attached to the outcome and having high expectations won't serve you. When you think about creating the life you desire, you will best serve yourself by training your mind and behaviour so that you can be in the moment as much as possible and let the outcome take care of itself.

CASE STUDY: AFFINITY GROUP

Jamie Lewis is the Managing Director of the Affinity Group, a company that offer mortgages, protection and alternative finance options.

Jamie reached out to me at a critical moment for his business; he was at a point where he thought he might lose all that he had worked for. I listened to his concerns and what was happening to the business and asked him three questions:

- Do you trust me?
- Will you commit to not attaching yourself to a fixed outcome?
- Will you do whatever it takes within legal, ethical and moral parameters?

He answered yes to all three questions and we got to work.

In his own words Jamie said, 'Our first meeting set the stall out for what he expected of me and he got straight to the core of the problems. This meant a restructure; it meant hard conversations and new skills. After only experiencing the rise, to have someone support me at this point was absolutely imperative to the business's survival.'

Did we know what we wanted as the ideal outcome? Yes, but when you undertake any kind of restructure, the key is to focus on just the next step, trust the process and detach from the outcome. Jamie did this and, as a result, he now runs a business that has doubled its turnover and has a thriving team.

Detaching from outcomes starts with who you are trying to be. Returning to the Be Do Have model, we grow up in a society that teaches us to want things. Then we work out what actions we need to take to get the things we want, thinking this will make us happy, successful and rich. This often fails.

When we detach ourselves from the outcome, we approach life differently. We decide who we want to be in life, then we decide what actions we need to take to become that person. The result – the riches, the success, the happiness – looks after itself.

Using a sporting example, imagine an athlete training for the Olympics. The athlete who decides to train as a champion, eat like a champion and behave like a champion, even before they win anything, detaches themselves from the outcome, focuses on the person they want to become and acts like that person.

Decide who you want to be and what you need to do to be that person, then use the NATO method to guide your actions.

28. Pebble ripples

Taking action is essential, but taking consistent, persistent action is the game changer. The closer together individual actions, the greater their compound effect.

When you throw a pebble into a lake, you see ripples that continue for a while and then fade away. If you throw another pebble ten minutes later, the first set of ripples have likely disappeared. But if you throw a second pebble ten seconds later, in the same place, the ripples of that second pebble will build upon the ripples of the first, and you get bigger ripples.

Imagine then if you threw a pebble into the lake every ten seconds; the ripples created by each pebble would build upon the ripples of the last until you start to create big waves. You're not throwing the pebbles any harder, or throwing bigger pebbles. All you are doing is being consistent, throwing pebble after pebble, with the same force.

We have this notion that to create a big impact in the world we have to make big statements and do big things. This is not always the case. If you are consistent in taking action and focus on the process, the result (the ripples) will follow.

Think of ten pebbles as ten tasks. All you need to do is put the same effort into each task, but you need to be consistent and throw these pebbles (ie complete these tasks) close enough together that there is a knock-on benefit. If you're consistent in what you do, the momentum will build and the impact you have in the world will be greater. It is the consistency not the magnitude of what you do that matters.

This kind of consistency also requires patience. It requires you to stay in the game. It requires you to not be attached to the outcome. It requires you to focus only on what you need to do, day in, day out. If you can do this, your impact on the world will be massive.

29. The grind

This is all about grit. There will be days you don't feel like doing anything, you can't be arsed, you just want to have a duvet day. This is fine every now and again, but if these moments happen more often than is ideal, you are going to struggle to maintain consistent action-taking and stay on your A-game. If you can push through these difficult moments, it's extremely satisfying.

The key is to recognise when you are in this type of slump. What I suggest is that you allow yourself some time in that slump. Not long. Ideally just a few minutes, an hour, maybe a day. Then, after that time has elapsed, you need to make a conscious decision to get back into action. This is the grind. It's about making a conscious choice to push on even when you don't feel like it. But not at all costs. Relentless pushing is a false economy. Listen to your body, your intuition, there will be times when it's good to push through when you don't want to and there will be times when you need to pause and rest before you get back in the game.

30. Creating the space for grace

I run a challenge with a select group of action-takers called the 7-Day Accountability Sprint (7DAS). The idea of this challenge is to pick a project you are procrastinating with, something you want to get done but hasn't become properly urgent yet. A project that you park in the 'when I have time' box. Guess what? You never have time. What happens is that the project becomes more urgent over time and you end up working on it under circumstances that don't serve you.

The 7DAS is designed to get this project over the line in seven days. Day three of the process is pivotal. It's the day that you usually fall behind on the project as you have overstated what you can do in a small space of time and set unrealistic targets for days one and two. On day three of a recent 7DAS I asked for feedback from the participants; I wanted to know what they were discovering about themselves and the process. One of the participants, Lesley Thomas, said something interesting.

At the time, she was on schedule. She had broken all the steps down into small tasks and was setting herself up for success. She was giving herself the 'space for grace' to ensure she not only completed the project but also stayed on top of all the other things she was doing that week.

This phrase perfectly captures why it's so important to appreciate that sometimes taking no action is taking intentional action. You are not being lazy; you're not procrastinating. Creating the space for grace is giving yourself an opportunity to reflect, to breathe, to plan, to recharge and to have time for creativity.

PART 2
PLAYING ON THE COURT

Now you have set the foundations in place, it's time to play. You are in the game. Watching from the sidelines, observing others and letting the world go by around you will only get you so far. Sooner or later you have to get on the court if you want your life to change.

In this part of the book, we will explore concepts, tactics and strategies for playing to win. If you have the *Win Your Game Planner*, you can use this to further improve your chances.

When you start to play, guess what? You'll win some games, you'll lose others. You will fall, and you will get back up. You may get hurt. Life and business is a game. You can make some of your own rules when you follow the core principles in this book.

Intentional Actions

31. Avoid a settled life

A settled life is an ordinary life. A life that you have accepted as your lot. A life where you have no ambition to grow, professionally or personally, and you feel either that you have achieved your potential or that you're happy enough not to. There is nothing wrong with feeling settled, but it is not the mindset of those playing their A-game.

At this point in the book, I'll give you a warning. You will have to make changes and many of them will be uncomfortable. Playing your A-game means living an exciting, unsettled life. Unsettled means you won't settle. When you settle, you compromise, you give up on things that seem either too hard or impossible to achieve. It doesn't have to be that way.

32. Can you do this?

Can you be someone who plays their A-game? I don't know. What I do know is that there is a strong correlation between people who commit, who take consistent action, who never give up, and people who succeed.

Now ask yourself a different question, not can you do this, but *will* you do this? When thinking about your answer, I want you to let go of two things, the *how* and the *when*. In order for you to play and be on top of your A-game, you should focus instead on the *why* and the *what*.

Be willing to let go of the how and the when, because you're not yet informed of the complete picture. Focusing on *when* you want to achieve puts you under unnecessary pressure. This doesn't mean you don't set parameters around short- and medium-term goals, or that there won't be tasks that are time sensitive, but that you don't fixate on timescales around the bigger picture.

When I started my business in 2007, I was coaching and training on a one-to-one basis, with a few corporate clients. I knew I wanted to create a worldwide impact, but I didn't know how I was going to do that. For the first four or five years, I still had no idea about the *how*, but the more people I networked with, the more resources I collated, the more informed I became, the more I started to piece together how it was possible. It was only in 2015 that I fully understood how I was going to create my vision.

As you take in all the concepts, strategies and ideas in this book and think about applying them to create your vision, let go of the how and the when and simply lean in to the ideas and the process. I promise you that the how will come to you, often at the most unexpected of times.

33. The intentional mindset

When I think about 'ordinary', I think about being average, about not standing out from the crowd, about settling for things in your life, about letting fear rule your decisions.

Carol Dweck explained the difference between the fixed mindset and the growth mindset.[12] The fixed mindset is what I would describe as being ordinary. Someone with an intentional mindset has a growth mindset with a little extra intention.

---

12   C Dweck, *Mindset: The new psychology of success* (Ballantine Books, 2007)

Below is how Carol Dweck differentiated between the fixed and growth mindsets:

Fixed Mindset	Growth Mindset
Avoids challenges	Embraces challenges
Gives up when obstacles appear	Persists to overcome obstacles
Making effort is fruitless	Effort is the path to mastery
Ignores criticism and feedback	Learns from criticism and feedback
Threatened by others' success	Finds lessons and inspiration from others' success

Adapted from C Dweck, *Mindset: The new psychology of success* (Ballantine Books, 2007)

When you have an ordinary, fixed mindset, you make low-level decisions. You allow the things that happen around you that are outside your control influence you, instead of taking control of the things you can influence. You resist taking action out of fear of judgement, fear of getting it wrong, fear of failure, fear of taking two steps back.

When you start to be intentional in every area of your life, you align your mindset with the actions you take, the conversations you have, the decisions you take. All of it becomes intentional and the results that you see in your life are surrounded by positive intent. When you start being intentional, you identify the things that you have some control over and you take ownership of those things. For example, your fitness, your health, your money and your relationships with your loved ones. You don't let things happen by chance; you take control, where you can, and then you let life happen. You accept the things that you cannot control. This is still being intentional, because you're not allowing things that you can do nothing about to worry you. Responsibility is part of this. Ownership is part of this. It requires an approach to life that accepts there is no such thing as a free lunch. No one is going to save you, to do everything for you. You control what you create.

When we get frustrated, it's often because of things we can't control that perhaps mean the results we want are not forthcoming. I have no idea what circumstances you're currently in. You might have 90% of the life you want, or just 10%, maybe even less. When you look at your life, you might think there are certain things you cannot change because either you don't have the resources, the opportunities or the support that you think you need. What's important in these moments is to focus on what you do have, what you can be grateful for, what you can do and start making micro changes in your life. When you start to make changes and be intentional with the actions you can take, even small ones, you get the ripple effect that we talked about earlier and everything else starts to gain momentum and require less effort.

That's the intentional mindset, beginning with the intent to take small, smart actions that you know will create momentum which in turn will maximise the results. Everything has a knock-on effect. What small wins can you find right now in your life? What can you be intentional around? Where have you got low-hanging fruit?

When you focus on these things, rather than the things you can't control or can't influence, the ordinary starts to become extraordinary, because you become intentional.

34. Control consistency

One of the first areas to look at when you're trying to live a non-negotiable life is your self-discipline. When you have self-discipline, the world opens up to you. Self-discipline is directly linked to your consistency.

We humans are easily distracted and the amount of information we are bombarded with every day through various media and platforms is astonishing. We have internal filters to block out information that we don't want to see, but the marketers battling for your attention will use every trick in the book to try and get your attention. All humans seek pleasure and avoid pain. We will be tempted by efforts to distract that utilise that knowledge. Those who are self-disciplined and not tempted by shiny objects, not influenced by outside forces trying to change their direction, are the ones that win the game. This is where your non-negotiable lifestyle, your self-discipline and your consistency protect you and keep you on your own path.

You need to be consistent in how you make decisions. You need to be consistent in avoiding temptation. You need to be consistent in your routine. You need to be consistent with your boundaries and you need to be able to say no. When a situation doesn't serve you, you need to be able to walk away. One of the things that highly self-disciplined people are great at is identifying what they can and can't control and letting go of the things they can't control. Things like other people's behaviours, their reactions, their expectations. If you are not self-disciplined it is easy to let these things influence you in a way that doesn't serve you.

Get a piece of paper and list all the things you know you can control and all the things you can't. Now ask yourself, if you had a non-negotiable lifestyle and felt empowered to say no to things without fear of offending or upsetting others, what would you say no to? If you could say yes to things that may upset or disappoint others but you know will serve you, what would you say yes to?

Self-discipline is a muscle you need to train because with focus, with structure and with discipline will come your freedom and with it that non-negotiable lifestyle. You are only one action, one decision, one moment away from freedom, but it requires consistency and control.

35. You are your best asset

Playing your A-game requires you to be at your best. We all have good days and bad days, but if you look after your best asset – which is yourself – you'll have more good than bad. Looking after your best asset means looking after your mind, your body and your spirit. By spirit, I mean your outlook on life, your vitality, your enthusiasm, your optimism.

How do you look after your mind? Reading books like this one is a start. Continue reading, watching and learning, finding inspiration, and seek out materials and resources that feed your mind and inspire optimism and positivity.

To look after your body, you need to exercise, meditate and eat healthily. In *Change Your Game* I talk about all the things you need to do to look after your body because without you being physically well, nothing works and you cannot reach your optimum performance level.

Finally, to look after your spirit and maintain a generally optimistic outlook on life, you need to get into your 'flow'. The concept of flow was first developed by Dr Mihaly Csikszentmihalyi, who went as far as saying that being in flow contributes to a life worth living.[13] When you're in your flow, everything is great, there's no need for you to even think about things. Wonderful things happen. But there are times when you're not in flow, when you're not feeling great. In those dark moments you need to feel for your optimism and your spirit, to try and find a place to be productive and look to the light – that's where you will grow. The best way to do that is to be grateful, to appreciate what you do have and not fixate on what you don't. Always look at the cup as half full; always look for the opportunity not the obstacle that's in front of you. Taking this approach will ensure that your best asset, yourself, is in an optimum state more often than not.

36. The power of mentoring

Mentoring is one of those things that is hard to explain the impact of, but once you experience it you know how powerful it can be. A mentor is somebody who you can talk to and obtain guidance, support and feedback. This might be on a one-to-one basis, or maybe as part of a group. The form that mentoring takes is less important to discuss than its power and what it gives you.

Mentoring unlocks your blind spots; it gives you perspectives you might never have considered; it unlocks potential within you that you might not have known

---

13   Dr M Csikszentmihalyi, *Flow: The psychology of engagement with everyday life* (HarperCollins, 1990)

you had. I don't know anyone who has reached their A-game without some element of mentoring, whether that's a paid coach or a trusted advisor who they just go to for counsel, or to talk through ideas.

CASE STUDY: ANDY LOPATA

I first met Andy Lopata on the professional speaker circuit. He is someone who I have a lot of respect for and look to learn from and be inspired by.

He is a great speaker and mentor to many within the corporate space, with a focus on building professional relationships. Over the years we have met at many events. Following a conversation at one such event, he reached out to me, interested in the coaching and mentoring I was offering.

Andy recognised that, even though he was a mentor to many, he could benefit from having a mentor himself. The power of mentoring is that it's not about training or learning in a direct sense, but about the relationship, about trust and holding a space of empowered accountability. This allowed Andy to step back from what he was looking to achieve in his business and gain another perspective. This was a big factor in helping his business survive the first fiscal quarter of the pandemic and supporting its subsequent growth over the course of several lockdowns. The mentoring relationship reminded Andy of things that he could action that would be highly effective, that tapped into his already well-connected network, things that were only a conversation away, but without that relationship the conversation wouldn't have happened.

The form and structure of mentoring can vary, but having a mentor of some kind is one of the most powerful, beneficial and revealing things you can do for yourself.

What makes a good mentor? There are a few things to look for:

1. **They are fantastic and insightful listeners.** Good mentors are active listeners, listening to not only what you say but what you don't say. They can unhook the problem before you even know it's there.

2. **They cut through the BS and get specific.** They are like a sharp knife, cutting away the debris and distraction to get to exactly the area you need help with. You might go to them looking for advice on X, Y, Z. They will talk things through with you and realise the issue is in fact just Y, you don't need to worry about X or Z, as they will resolve once you've dealt with Y.

3. **They are completely honest with you**, about what you're capable of and your limitations; they're honest about timescales and your capacity. But they also won't allow these to hinder you, they will help you to understand how to work around or break through those limitations.

4. **They will hold you accountable.** They won't let you go about your business unchecked; they will

follow up on what you've talked about, they will ensure that you've done whatever you agreed to. They are as invested in your development as you are.

5. **They're trustworthy.** There's an enormous amount of trust in the mentoring relationship because your mentor is the one person you're going to be completely honest with because this is essential for progress. They are invested in but emotionally detached from your success. They're empathetic about issues you face but won't let you be swallowed by them.

If you're lucky enough to have a mentor, make sure you use them. If you don't have a mentor, find one. Who do you like? Who do you respect? Who do you admire? It could be somebody you know personally, somebody you follow on social media, somebody you recently met. Figure out who that person is and go and speak to them.

37. Discipline, sacrifice and integrity

Discipline, sacrifice and integrity are linked. I've already highlighted the importance of self-discipline when you live a non-negotiable lifestyle, but we haven't yet touched on sacrifice and integrity. Sacrifice can sometimes be considered a punishment. Instead, I suggest you look at it as letting go of things – perhaps an opinion, a perspective, or a frame of reference – in order to play a different game. We make sacrifices all the time, even if we might not know it. Integrity is how you choose to live your life. It's showing up and doing what you say you'll do, what you intend to do, and still doing it when no one is watching.

How are discipline, sacrifice and integrity linked? It comes back to your values. For you to truly live in accordance with your values, this will involve a degree of discipline and sacrifice. Your values might include healthy living, being kind to others and prioritising family. Healthy living requires exercise; prioritising family means making the time for them when they want and need it. Living according to your values gives you integrity, it's you walking the walk not just talking the talk, but it will require you to make sacrifices, which takes discipline.

You need discipline to exercise three or four times a week, whether you feel like it or not; you need to commit to it and will have to sacrifice other things to honour that commitment. You might have to give up certain foods; you might have to say no to going out sometimes in order for you to be true to your values and have integrity.

Unfortunately, we live in a society that wants instant rewards, instant reactions, instant gratification. We open up our phones, we go on social media, we click and scroll to get a reward. But to play your A-game, in order for you to get what you want in life, you're going to have to make sacrifices.

Consider elite athletes, they have to train. They have to give up a lot of things, including socialising, and have to be very disciplined in life to go after what they want. Muhammad Ali is often quoted as saying, 'I hated every minute of training, but I said, "Don't quit. Suffer now and live the rest of your life as a champion."' He hated training, but knew that it was something he had to do to be a champion and achieve the success he craved. This demonstrates how discipline, sacrifice and integrity are linked.

The question you now need to answer is where in your life do you need to be disciplined? What do you need to sacrifice to have integrity and live according to your values? When you see the link to integrity you realise that actually being disciplined and making sacrifices doesn't mean you have to give up on life, that you have to live a boring life, that you can't enjoy yourself. It means that you live your best life, the life you want to live, a life that you value. It means you're prepared to do the work now to get a greater reward later on. That's the mindset of someone playing their A-game.

38. Do what you say, say what you do

A big part of integrity is doing what you say you'll do. In my corporate job, I did what I needed to do, maybe just enough to ensure I got the results I needed, to ensure my employer was satisfied, even though I loved what I was doing. For many in the corporate world it's exactly the same.

When I started my business over twelve years ago, for the first few years it felt pretty similar to my corporate job, from a discipline and productivity perspective. I was 'doing the job' but not with the complete conviction it needed. Looking back, this was probably because I was afraid of failing. I hadn't been made redundant from my corporate job, or been sacked. I left of my own accord, so the pressure to do well was massive. In response to this pressure, I think I played it safe a little. From the outside, my business looked great, but I knew I wasn't going in all guns blazing, giving it my all.

I realised that the way I was doing things was just as important as what I was doing. As a performance psychologist coaching others to ensure they maximised their performance, was I doing myself what I was encouraging others to do? Was I practising what I preached? The simple answer was no, certainly not all the time. This didn't work for me from the point of view of my values and integrity. For me, saying I was going to do something meant I was going to do it. No compromise. I made it non-negotiable.

When you commit to no compromise, it's amazing how much your life improves. When you make this shift your integrity increases, because all of a sudden you will think twice about the commitments you make, you manage expectations better, not only your own but those of others.

Your productivity will go through the roof because once you commit you don't want to be seen as someone who doesn't keep their promises. You don't want to be seen as someone who says one thing and does another. Even if no one is watching, *you* know.

When you are playing your A-game and you start to meet and interact with more successful people, you become more confident in saying no and knowing what you're not prepared to commit to. If you say yes all the time you are likely to compromise on your values and commit to things that you can't deliver, or not to your standards. As a consequence, people might start to see you as someone they can't rely on.

Ask yourself, what will it take for you to create a life where you say what you do and then do what you say, with no excuses? This goes back to living a non-negotiable life. Playing your A-game means that whatever is going around in the world, you learn to adapt to circumstances outside your control, to ensure you still deliver what you said you would deliver. You adapt, you pivot, you find a way through.

If you can do this, you will create even greater value for yourself, because people take notice of those who turn up when they say they will, and come to rely on them. So if you say it, do it.

39. Create order

There's sometimes a perception that when you're organised, when you've got things lined up and in order, that life can be boring, stifling and suffocating, with no freedom, flexibility or room for manoeuvre. In fact, the opposite is true. When you create order in your life, when you organise things that are within your control, when you are disciplined, when you plan and then execute your plans, life becomes effortless.

Stacking dominoes takes organisation and planning. Imagine you've got a thousand dominoes. Your goal is to, with a single effort, knock every domino down. The execution is quick and simple, the result huge. Actually knocking them down is very little effort at all; but to organise them in such a way that a single, insignificant effort is all that's required, takes planning and careful thought.

If you've got certain systems and processes in place, perhaps ones that are automated, then you've got a degree of order in your life. Work with non-negotiables, set routines, great habits, and effective and efficient decision-making skills and that order will give you greater control. That means that when you start playing your game, the A-game, when life happens, the negative impact won't be as bad. If the majority of your life is within your control due to good habits, systems and processes, you will be on top of your game.

When you start taking actions to bring about certain results, but you haven't got a solid foundation in place, you're trying to build on shallow, rocky ground and you're leaving a lot to luck. Check your foundations before you build, and get everything lined up before you get started. As with when you build a house, it's what you can't see, the foundations, that makes the building stable and secure.

The same is true in life. When someone has got their A-game on point, they seem to get all the opportunities, all the results, they seem to have light leading their way. It all looks effortless, easy. What you don't see behind the scenes are the foundations they've put in place. The years of hard graft. The order they have created. You might see the person with a six pack. What you haven't seen is the previous 365 days where they've gone to the gym in the morning, they've eaten food you wouldn't want and sacrificed nights out. You only see the end result. That person has put the dominoes in order. You see the person who's had 'overnight success', but you don't see the ten years leading up to it.

Trusting The Process

40. Never be late

I'm going to challenge you to commit to something that you instinctively might think is not possible: never, ever be late. I mean late for anything – an appointment, a project, a phone call, a meeting – anything. Your mind might immediately be going, 'Hang on, if I take public transport, what if the bus doesn't show up? What if the train is late? What if my flight is cancelled?' You're right, there are many things outside your control that could prevent you from being on time. Life happens and sometimes the best laid plans go out of the window. I'm sure you can think of a whole list of examples. But I would argue that these occasions are fewer than you may care to admit.

What I want you to understand is when you decide and empower yourself to say, 'I will never be late, for anything', what kind of person do you then need to become? What areas in your life are you going to have to look at, for there to be a chance of this happening? How much more disciplined and structured do you need to be to make this a reality? How can you make the commitment, to yourself and to others, to never be late?

First, you need to become someone with a high level of integrity. That's now not just about being on time, it's about how you run your life. When we are late for something, it's usually because we haven't planned ahead, we've underestimated a task and now we're playing catch-up.

The two things we all want more of are money and time. You can get more money, depending on what you are prepared to do and how risk averse you are. Time is something we can't get more of, it's finite. You can't stop it and you can't save it for later. With that in mind, it's amazing how much time is wasted through lack of discipline and a lack of respect for ourselves and for others.

When you commit to never being late, three things happen. One, your self-awareness increases. When you make this commitment, you start to be more organised, more disciplined, more aware of the impact that you have on other people when you're late. You start to think beyond what you want to do and look at the bigger picture of how you interact with others and the world and what that says about you. Two, your energy increases. The amount of energy you have is directly related to how you are feeling. When you have more energy, you get more done in a shorter space of time. You are more focused, there are fewer distractions; you are not looking for excuses or ways to procrastinate.

The A-game player does not accept mundane excuses from themselves or from others. We are too forgiving and too accommodating when other people are late for no other reason than they are not organised enough.

If there is a genuine reason for being late, people under-stand. When 'the bus was late' or 'traffic was bad' becomes a default excuse and you're constantly late, it becomes about self-awareness and self-discipline. The kind of excuse that rolls off the tongue without any awareness is intended simply to justify an action. What you really mean is you forgot, something came up, you got distracted. You probably know someone who you can guarantee will always be late. They won't ring on time, they won't turn up on time, they will just do whatever. Maybe you accept that behav-iour as standard from them – do not accept that from yourself. Never, ever be late.

The third thing that happens is you are positioned in other people's minds as someone with high integrity, someone who is organised and can be relied upon. That is a powerful place to be. There are people in the world who will conspire to throw you off your A-game. I guarantee that when you start saying, 'I'll never be late', everyone will be looking out for you to be late even just once, by just one minute.

Again it's about consistency and how people see you. If you say that you will never be late and people believe that you're never late, that's the standard which you set, the conditions you give them. That's then what they expect from you; what that does, in turn, is improves their standards and their behaviour in return.

If you want to play your A-game, never be late. It is a great benchmark for the level of integrity you possess and is something that everyone can see and understand when you uphold it. Start by committing to never be late for anything, whether important or not, for a week, then a month, and see how your life changes and how others respond to you.

41. Confidence vs conviction

You need both confidence and conviction to play your A-game. But which comes first? Do you need confidence to have conviction? Or does your conviction lead to confidence?

There is no right or wrong way. For some people, it's confidence first, for others it's conviction. What I have found, though, is that confidence, for the majority of people, is influenced by emotion. Emotion is often triggered by outside events, things outside your control, things that you don't expect.

When we're talking about playing your A-game, we're talking about what you can control. You can control your conviction. Your conviction is your dedication to the cause. Your conviction is how you turn up for the event. Your conviction is the way you are as an individual. Your conviction is your firmly held beliefs.

From my personal experience, my own performance and my working with other entrepreneurs and leaders and people who are looking for success consistently, your conviction is something you can choose and control. When you have conviction about what you want to create, even if you don't know how to get there, your confidence will be raised. What happens then is you start getting results. Some results you want, some you don't and some you don't expect.

I've talked about NATO in this book and in *Change Your Game*, where you focus on process not outcome. When you have conviction about how you want to turn up each day, you are focused on the process. You take a step forward, then another, irrespective of outcome.

As long as you stay on your path, stay in your lane, keep your vision clear, surround yourself with the right people and refuse to give up, your confidence will incrementally increase. There will be days that challenge you and your confidence will dip. You will have ups and downs and it may come in waves, but over a period of time your confidence will increase. This is down to having conviction about where you want to get to. You cannot rely on your confidence alone, as this is mood dependent, which is potentially uncontrollable. But when you have a conviction about what you want to create in your life, what and who you want to serve and the wealth you want to create – whether that be financial, spiritual, emotional or physical – you are entering the realms of the 1% of this world. These people have complete conviction and do not rely on their day-to-day mood for their confidence.

42. No Plan B

Not having a Plan B is about a mindset. It's based on a philosophy that those playing the right game, their game, don't have a Plan B. What they have is Plan A, and they make that plan work. They might approach it in different ways, but they keep to the plan.

You might think that having a Plan B isn't about having a second vision, and that's what's important – the core vision is what you should focus on and as long as you don't compromise on that, a Plan B of how to get there isn't a big deal. But if you have a Plan B, part of you, even if subconsciously, is not playing full-out, is compromising on Plan A. Plan A is what is going to get you your riches, your wealth, your success, your impact. Plan B might do, but not in the way you want to do it. A Plan B gives you a cushion, an out, a back-up, an easier option.

The fact that you're reading this book means you want to play your own game. That means you have Plan A and only Plan A. You make Plan A non-negotiable. You go out and do whatever it takes. You might have to make adjustments, you might have to pivot, you might have to take two steps back. You might need more resources, you might have to get creative, but you do not give up on Plan A. Don't give yourself that way out. Having a no Plan B mindset means you're fully committed to Plan A. You're all in and there's no compromise.

43. Point of no return

You have reached the point of no return. You have made a mental, physical and spiritual commitment to yourself that *this is it*. Everything now is a choice, because you have the tools. Not many have done or can do this. We are so conditioned to accept the ordinary, the status quo, that to allow yourself to break away from your limiting story and transition to a higher level of living is tough.

This is the way of entrepreneurial and inspired leaders. Whatever lies ahead, you find a way. Your cup is always half full, no matter what the situation. Lead by example; be an example for yourself and for others. Playing your A-game means you are living the example you want others to follow.

You are looking to transition from an ordinary life to an intentional life. In a nutshell, living an ordinary life means you let life happen *to* you; living an intentional life means you take control of all areas, and life happens *for* you. You are responding to everything and not reacting to anything. You are intentional in everything you do.

Before you started your journey of self-improvement and developing your entrepreneurial and leadership mindsets, before you picked up this book and decided to play your game, you were living an ordinary life. Was that serving you? Were you consistently getting the results you wanted? Did you learn from your failures? Did you complain in the face of bad fortune? How self-aware were you?

Moving to an intentional way of life, you are now in control. What does this look like? It means being intentional in everything you do from the moment you get up to how you choose to behave in each moment; how you respond to others; how you map out what you do each day; the plans you make for yourself and the actions you take to make them happen; how you choose the people you surround yourself with, so that they serve you rather than drain you. It means the standards you set yourself being non-negotiable.

An ordinary life happens *to* you. You wake up when you feel like it; you see how the day unfolds; you become busy doing things that seem important, but don't actually get you anywhere. You mean to get back to people, but you just don't find the time. You plan to stay fit, but you can't be bothered. You don't care what you eat and grab something as you go. At work, the actions you take are not in line with your plans and you use lack of time and money as excuses for why your grand plan never happens.

A day becomes a week and before you know it, a month has gone by and you haven't achieved even 10% of what you set out to do. Now you have the choice to live an intentional life and take back control. Have a vision for your life and business, create a road-map for how to get there and then take micro actions every day to make it happen.

At the centre of all of this is self-care. Without health, nothing matters. Being intentional does not mean letting yourself burn out. On the contrary, you should be full of energy, because of three things:

- **You know what you want.** You take action every day to get it and feel good as a result of taking these micro actions.

- **You create momentum.** The more you create over time, the less effort it takes for you to get the same results. Living an intentional life allows momentum to build faster because you are not letting things slip.

- **You are 'luckier'.** Things start happening to you that seem like good fortune, but they are rewards for living an intentional rather than an ordinary life.

44. Your achievement timeline

It doesn't matter how old you are, or what stage of life you are at, you have achieved some great things in your life. It's easy to forget what you have achieved and the learnings, lessons, skills and insights you may have gained from all your achievements.

The achievement timeline exercise will help you identify and map out all the significant achievements and lessons in your life so far. Take a blank piece of paper. At the top of the page, write your age, then halve your age and write that a quarter of the way down the page. Now count back five years from that age and for that five-year period ask yourself two questions:

- What were your three greatest achievements?

- What were your three greatest lessons?

Once you have done this, count up five years from half your current age and repeat the exercise. Do this in five-year sections until you reach your age now. See my example exercise below. When you have finished, you will have a list of achievements and lessons you have gained throughout your life.

THE AGE YOU ARE NOW			
PLUS 5 YEARS			
PLUS 5 YEARS			
HALF YOUR AGE			
MINUS 5 YEARS FROM HALF YOUR AGE			

At any given stage of life we look at what we want and the resources we have and we base our actions and mindset on this limited information. With this knowledge of the most significant achievements and lessons throughout your life, celebrate what you have done. There will have been times (and there will be times again) where you faced some sort of adversity that might put your current challenges in perspective. Pick out a particular achievement or lesson – what was your mindset then? How did you overcome fear at that time? Looking back on the periods of your life where it seemed there was no way out, or you couldn't see a good outcome, what happened in the end? Whatever the actual outcome, you lived to fight another day. Now draw on all those experiences and lessons and use them to strengthen your A-game today.

Your A-Game

45. Your message to the world

Live in a way that reflects what you want the world to be. Too many of us wait for others to change or make the first move. If you want the world to be a certain way, then do something about it. Your life is a message to the world. It is often said that people don't remember what you do or say, but how you make them feel. Like it or not, your life is a message to the world. What message are you sending? Is it the one you want?

Let me make this clear, this is not about becoming a humanitarian hero, or a UN leader, but someone who lives by their values and is true to their word.

Mahatma Gandhi is said to have implored us to be the change we wanted to see in the world. Would you like to see more compassion? Then you must show more compassion, without compromise. Would you like more people to live with integrity? Then you must live with absolute integrity. Would you like people to keep their word? Then keep yours.

When you start with your own life, you start to see the kind of world you want. Your life is a message to the world, make sure it's the message you want. My message to the world is that I want everyone to live the life they desire, so I work to create that every day. I want everyone to keep their word, so I keep mine. I want people to never give up on what they believe in, so I never will.

46. Your values are your anchor

Do you know what your values are, what you live by? If you're not sure, there's an exercise at the end of this section that will help you identify them. It's amazing, when you start doing the work on yourself for personal development, you identify what's important to you and see how those values turn up in your life, and things start to fall into place.

It's easy to see when someone's not truly living their values because there's a lot of frustration in their life; there's anger, there's disappointment, there's friction, there's resistance. When you live by your values, these frustrations evaporate, and your actions align with your inner anchor. When you understand your values and the actions you take align with your vision, you are playing your A-game.

I completed the values exercise myself and identified the four core values I want to live my life by. These same values govern my businesses:

- **Growth**: I am always thinking about what I need to do to grow, how I can help others grow. If I'm not growing, I'm going backwards.

- **Simplicity**: If I can't explain it to a ten-year-old, it's too complicated. It's not about being simplistic, but about making complex concepts and strategies simple to understand.

- **Excellence**: This is about striving for the best and always maintaining high standards, never settling for anything less, but not being held back by perfectionism.

- **Collaboration**: I strive to create win-win-win situations with partners, experts and influencers to make a greater impact.

Now it's your turn to work through the exercise below to discover your top values. Once you've identified your values, you will be able to see if they show up in the work that you do, in the life that you lead and in the results that you get. Once you reach a point where your values are aligned, it's a game changer.

Values exercise

What are your values, the things that you consider to be important and worthwhile in life? These are your highest priorities and driving forces.

In relation to your career, values are what give purpose to your job or business. You bring your deeply held values and beliefs to your work in any organisation in which you work. The effort, commitment and motivation that a person brings to a job is in direct proportion to the values that they perceive the organisation to represent.

The first thing to establish is your core value. From the list below, select the ten things that are most important to you – in work and in life – as guides for how to behave, or as components of a principled way of life. Feel free to add any of your own to this list.

List of values

Accomplishment	Financial gain	Problem solving
Accountability	Flair	Progress
Accuracy	Freedom	Prosperity
Achievement	Friendship	Public service
Advancement	Fun	Punctuality

Adventure	Global view	Purity
Affection	Goodness	Quality of work
Arts	Goodwill	Recognition/status
Beauty	Gratitude	Regularity
Calm	Growth	Religion
Challenge	Hard work	Reputation
Change	Harmony	Resourcefulness
Cleanliness	Having a family	Respect for others
Close relationships	Helping others	Responsibility
Collaboration	Helping society	Responsiveness
Commitment	Honesty	Results-oriented
Communication	Honour	Romance
Community	Independence	Safety
Competence	Influencing others	Satisfying others
Competition	Inner peace – calm, quietude	Security
Concern for others	Innovation	Self-reliance
Continuous improvement	Integrity	Self-respect
Cooperation	Intellectual status	Serenity
Coordination	Involvement	Service – to others, society
Country – love of/patriotism	Justice	Simplicity
Creativity	Knowledge	Skill

Continued

Customer satisfaction	Leadership	Sophistication
Decisiveness	Location	Speed
Delighting being	Love	Spirit in life
Democracy	Loyalty	Stability
Discipline	Meaning	Standardisation
Discovery	Merit	Status
Ease of use	Money	Strength
Ecological awareness	Motivation	Success
Economic security	Nature	Systemisation
Effectiveness	Openness	Teamwork
Efficiency	Order – tranquility/ stability	Time
Equality	Peace/Non-violence	Timeliness
Ethical practice	Perfectionism, eg attention to detail	Tolerance
Excellence	Personal growth	Tradition
Excitement	Physical challenge	Tranquillity
Fairness	Pleasure	Trust
Faith	Positive attitude	Truth
Fame	Power	Unity
Family	Practicality	Variety
Fast living	Preservation	Wealth
Feeling	Privacy	Wisdom

Once you have identified your top ten, cut those down to the five most important. Then down to three. Finally, get rid of two more. The one that is left is your core value.

47. Become unstoppable

When you decide to become unstoppable, you create a shift in your beliefs, feelings, thoughts and actions. When we are moving forward there will be many obstacles and challenges. Our survival instincts will say, 'Play it safe, do what you need to do, don't take any risks.' Three things in particular slow you down or make you stop:

- Procrastination

- Overwhelm

- Overthinking

All are success killers; they don't serve you when playing your A-game. How you deal with each of these starts with your mindset, followed by taking just one micro action to create momentum. Let's look at them in turn.

Procrastination should not be confused with planning, taking time out or doing research. You know when you are procrastinating. It's avoidance. Maybe the deadline isn't tight enough; maybe the reason behind the task isn't important enough in that moment; or maybe you are afraid that you won't get the result you are looking for, so you allow yourself to be distracted.

Overwhelm can be avoided if you focus your time and energy. When you collapse a series of tasks together, trying to work on multiple projects simultaneously and move from one thing to another without any perspective or priority, everything becomes urgent. Everything you do is important (if it wasn't, why would you be doing it?), but not everything is urgent. With good structure and planning, most of your tasks need not be in the urgent category.

Focus on small actionable tasks. We often overestimate what we can achieve in a day, but underestimate what we can do in a week and in a month. You can overcome this by committing to doing three small but intentional things every day. I promise if you do this you'll get more done in one week than you ever have before. It is when you think, 'I've got twenty things to do today' that things become overwhelming. Identifying small actionable tasks is the key to keeping things manageable while remaining highly productive. In the scenario of creating a course, you've got to create the website, the emails, the copy, all those big things. Then you tell the market about your new course – but what happens if the market doesn't want to know? Whereas, if you were to send one email today saying, 'If I did this and it was available in a month's time, would you be interested?' and no one replies saying yes, you've saved yourself a lot of wasted time. Breaking things down into smaller tasks allows you to readjust quickly.

Stephen Covey's Eisenhower Matrix is a great tool to deal with overwhelm and preventing a long 'to do' list.[14] It encourages you to understand your tasks with regards to two categories – 'urgent' and 'important', then separate tasks further into 'Do', 'Schedule', 'Delegate' and 'Delete' depending on timing and significance. It allows you to assess and organise your ongoing workload, to screen jobs that should not be your responsibility and to reduce urgent work so you gain greater control over your time and focus.

When you accept that not everything is equally as important and urgent, and you accept that you get more done in the long term by doing fewer things at one time in the short term, you can prevent overwhelm. The compound impact of this is increased confidence, greater efficiency and working smarter.

Don't confuse overthinking with thinking. Thinking is good, overthinking isn't. You overthink when you worry excessively about future and dwell on the past. Both are destructive thought patterns and don't serve you in any way. Knowing this and doing something about it, though, are two different things.

---

14 S Covey, *The 7 Habits of Highly Effective People* (Simon & Schuster, 2017)

To prevent overthinking, catch your thoughts – notice when you are having incessant thoughts about something and ask yourself: is this serving me? If it isn't, try and replace those worries with a more empowering thought. Don't overthink your overthinking though, just try and counter it, without expectation.

Another way to tackle overthinking is to get out of your head. Listen to your body, listen to your feelings, take some time out and focus on something completely different. Then you can return to the issue later, with fresh eyes. Go back to your why. What's the big picture? What is the reason you do what you do? Step back from the finer detail and gain some perspective.

48. The more you fail the more you learn

Whether or not you believe that failing means learning will depend on how many times you've failed and succeeded. We never plan to fail, but of course it happens.

We often fail when we try new things, when we push out of our comfort zones, when things don't go to plan.

History is littered with successful people who have failed. If you want to play your A-game, you cannot avoid failure. Thomas Edison made thousands of lightbulbs before he got one that worked. Steve Jobs was fired from the company *he* founded. Bill Gates was a Harvard dropout.

Success means different things to different people, so does failure. Some see failure as a form of success, because where else can they go from there except up? You could say that failure gives you freedom, freedom to fail again or, more likely, to succeed.

If there is an area of your life where you don't feel you have been successful, this doesn't necessarily mean you have failed in that area.

CASE STUDY: LAURA AND BARRY

Laura and Barry are business partners and life partners and run Rock Solid, a health and wellbeing business. I have known both for a number of years; we speak on and off and I have helped them with their business.

Business is tough at the best of times and there were many times for Laura and Barry where the results they were looking for were not forthcoming. This was not for want of trying. They were giving great value, were always generous with their expertise and had good systems in place.

There were a number of moments where they considered walking away from the business as it had become relentless. But it wasn't in their nature to give up. They never complained and were always looking for the lessons they could learn from each failure.

When we started working together on the Change Your Game Accelerator, in Laura's words they had lost sight of their vision, mission and values. They decided that they would give Rock Solid a year; if they hadn't turned it around by then, they would end it. But they knew that

> if they learned from their mistakes, played their A-game and kept trying and growing they would be successful. They did and they are. As a result of embracing their failures and working on their inner game, they and their business have gone from strength to strength.

The more you fail, the more you learn. That's just the way it is. You learn when you succeed, too, but the opportunities for reflection you get from failure are much more valuable. This is because when you're operating from a position of success, it's a position of strength. You assume that all is well, so there is less likelihood of you contemplating a change. At the point of failure, you are forced to reflect. You have to reassess your actions to see what needs to change so that you don't fail again. This requires a mindset shift. You are working your mindset muscles and when you work any muscle, it grows.

We tend not to work on ourselves, our mindset and our emotional intelligence as standard. More often than not, the time that people 'do the work' on themselves is when they've failed, because it's associated with pain. More people take paracetamol to relieve pain than take vitamins to prevent pain and maintain health. The best time to do the work on ourselves is when things are going well. You are filling up your tank so that when life happens and you meet failures and challenges, you are in a better place to deal with them. Prevention is better than cure but in both scenarios, there are opportunities to learn, grow and evolve.

When you fail, don't worry. Ask yourself, what can you learn from this? Did the actions you took align with your mindset? If your mindset and attitude was a little cautious, a little apprehensive, maybe your actions were too. Did you play full-out? Did you give yourself the best chance of success?

Many people don't learn from failure, because they don't do all they can. They do just enough to alleviate the pain. This is giving up too early, missing the opportunity to learn the big lesson. When you see successful people, know that they have probably had many failures. If you get the opportunity to, ask them what they've learned from their biggest failures. The insights you will gain from this conversation will be invaluable.

49. Resilience

To learn from your failures and play your A-game, you need resilience. Resilience builds strength and gives you a sense of perspective. It shows you how good you are and how good you can be. You only know how resilient you are when you're confronted with a challenge.

When you start to play the game that you want to play in life, you will inevitably face obstacles. This is just part of the game and resilience is a part of your armoury. The only way you'll know how resilient you are is to be confronted with a challenge. But there are things you can do to build resilience:

- **Change your language and your narrative**, how you talk about yourself and what you say about a situation. When you're confronted with an obstacle or challenge in your life, use positive not negative language about it, lean in and embrace it.

- **Face reality.** It is what it is. Sometimes we look at a situation and we want it to be something it's not. All that does is create upset, worry and frustration. If you see every situation for what it is, you are much more empowered to face that reality.

- **Be kind to yourself and show compassion.** Whether something was your fault or someone else's doing, be kind to yourself and others in any situation. This increases your positive energy and makes you much more productive.

- **Reach out to your network.** Don't ever feel that reaching out to your network for support when you're not feeling great is a bad thing. You will find that other people can relate to you and have probably been through similar situations; let them help build your resilience.

- **Take action.** Whether that's making a phone call, getting something ticked off your to do list, just *do* something, anything. When you take action, you realise that you are capable, you do have strength – keeping in motion, even if you've slowed down, is resilience.

Building your resilience is building your superpowers. There will come a point in your life, when you're playing your game, when you won't compromise, when you want more and you truly lean in to what is available to you. This comes with challenges, as I have explained; being resilient means taking responsibility for your actions, your thinking and your attitude – resilience is your superpower.

50. Simple but not easy

Many of the things talked about in this book are fairly simple, but they are not easy. That is a good and a bad thing. Good, in that it doesn't require you to have a degree or any special talent. Bad, for the same reason. If you did need a special talent or some kind of qualification, you would have the perfect excuse not to implement any of my recommendations. But you don't. You have no excuse.

Most of what you need to do now to play your game is simple, but it's not easy. If it's not easy, does that mean it's hard? Yes and no. Yes, because often you won't get immediate results that you can use to measure your progress. Yes, because it requires consistency and discipline to get to the point where you see results and you may have to deal with a challenging internal dialogue. 'Why bother? You aren't good enough. Who do you think you are? It will take too long, and you might fail anyway.' This stuff can be hard to deal with.

But then no, it's not hard, because, having read this book, you know exactly what you need to do. If you can remember the NATO method and can take action without attaching yourself to a fixed outcome, you will find a lot of the ideas in this book not only simple but easy to implement.

By nature, humans are lazy. When you think about committing to playing a bigger game, to unleashing your potential and creating the life you desire, the immediate thought is that it's going to be hard. And when something is hard, there's more chance of failure, more chance that you won't get the result you want. When it's hard, it could take longer than you want it to.

If you knew it would be easy, how would that change your mindset? If we believe something is easy, we don't overthink it, we just get on with it. If something is easy, we know there's a higher chance of success. We don't let our internal chatter get in the way.

Let me put this to you: it's not easy, it's not hard, it just is. That's the absolute truth. It just is. Because one person's impossible is another person's possible. Part of your journey to committing to playing your game is a change in your mindset, away from thinking some things are impossible and some are possible. First fix your mindset, then find the right strategy, then take action. It's not rocket science.

If you approach the task in hand with the view that 'it is what it is', without worrying about whether it's going to be hard or easy, you will succeed. If everything was easy, half the things that have been achieved and created in this world wouldn't have happened. We like a challenge. We need obstacles, resistance, problems to solve. This is where we test and discover our true potential. This is how we grow. These challenges push us to the next level. That's what playing your A-game is all about. So stop worrying about whether things are going to be easy or hard, just approach every opportunity, every challenge, every problem for what it is, and rise to it.

51. Act like a gold medallist

I want to try a thought experiment now. Imagine you are ten years old and you're told that you have the talent and potential to be an Olympic athlete. Let's say a 100-metre sprinter, for example. The people around you, your mentors and coaches, say that in order to fulfil your potential and ambition, you have to live a certain way. You've got to live as if you are already a gold medal athlete. You have the talent, you have the ability, they have seen the potential in you, but they also know that for you to actually win that gold medal you're going to have to commit to a certain lifestyle. You have to commit to being a certain type of person.

If you met someone who was training to be an Olympic athlete but who hadn't yet won a gold medal, what kind of lifestyle would you expect them to have? What would their life look like? You'd probably expect to them waking up early in the morning, eating the right food, training every day, listening to their mentors. You'd expect them to be structured and disciplined and to turn up each day in a serious and focused state of mind. The Olympics is held every four years, so they have to live this way for four years without any immediate reward for or validation of their efforts. They must focus on ensuring they do what they need to do each day, each week, each month to be ready for the starting line. The athlete who is playing their A-game does not wait to win the gold medal before they act like a gold medal athlete. They know that to win that gold medal, they have to live and act like they have already got it. That's what playing your game means.

The strategies, tactics and insights in this book are based on the assumption that you believe you will succeed. That you behave like you've already got what you're aiming for, like whatever it is you're trying to achieve is inevitable, like the result doesn't matter because you know you're going to get it. This is again about not being attached to the outcome. The elite athletes, the top people in any field, industry or sport, if you look at what they do day to day, they act as if the prize is already won.

Act like a gold medallist even before you've won the medal. Then do and be all you can to realise the result that you know is inevitably yours.

The Power Of Accountability

52. What accountability can do

Accountability, for me, is the ultimate game changer. Humans are born to survive, not to thrive. At the basic level, to survive we need air, food, water and sleep. That's it. Back when we had to hunt for food, we had no choice but to get on with it. We didn't have distractions, we didn't overthink things, we didn't have a million other things we could do. All we needed and wanted to do was survive.

In order to play your A-game you need to take it up a level, you need to thrive. A small percentage of people can do this consistently on their own. Another small percentage of people will never thrive, irrespective of their mindset, their environment or what resources you offer them. The fact that you are reading this book suggests you're not one of these people.

Aside from these two small groups of people, perhaps 90% of us want to thrive but, for whatever reason – mindset, resources, environment – we are not able to do so consistently. The key word here is 'consistently'. We can all thrive in moments, in short bursts, but doing this consistently throughout your life is a different thing altogether.

Accountability is one of the secrets to consistently thriving. Why is it that we know what to do, and we know how to do it, yet we are still not getting stuff done? Often it comes down to there being nothing, or no one, holding us accountable for what we've said we will do.

Accountability is beneficial in a whole variety of ways. It helps to eliminate distractions. As we know, life will happen. You are never completely ready and things will happen to you, good, bad and neutral. When you have accountability there is something or someone external to you that gets you focused. This helps to cut through distractions and get you focused. Pride is also a factor when there's a third party involved, or public exposure. Not wanting to lose face is often a powerful enough force to make distractions a lower priority.

Accountability helps you manage your energy better. With someone else checking in on your progress, you have greater clarity on what you need to complete this week, this month. This clarity on exactly what you need to do stops you from feeling overwhelmed and conserves your energy. Overwhelm can be paralysing, then you feel guilty for not taking any action, which is draining, leaving you trying to work with an empty tank. You might end up burning the midnight oil and then struggle to wake up in the morning and before you know it, it's Wednesday and you've achieved nothing. When your energy is low, you are less productive. Accountability, and the clarity it gives you, enables you to focus and maintain your energy.

A valuable aspect of accountability is concrete deadlines. We all have stuff to do; we'll probably set ourselves a loose deadline but then something happens and you have an excuse to miss it. There will always be something outside of your control that could impact your deadline. When someone is keeping you accountable, you will set concrete deadlines and they will hold you to them and not accept mundane excuses. Again, there is an element of pride in hitting those deadlines. You don't want to be the one that doesn't do it, the one always coming up with excuses.

I heard a great phrase, 'You might be on the right track, but if you are standing still you're going to get run over.' In a similar line of thought, you might be moving fast, looking like you're doing lots of activity, but if you're moving in the wrong direction, you're getting nowhere. With accountability, you're constantly being challenged with questions like, 'Is that really where you want to go? Is that really what you want to do?'

This kind of feedback and constructive criticism helps you to formulate a winning strategy. When you have a third party involved who is not emotionally invested in the process, it's easier to evaluate, test, measure and adjust.

Accountability helps you to create a better mental and physical environment. Your environment hugely influences your performance. Think about it, 80% of the exercise you do in the gym you could do at home, so why do we go to the gym? Because of the environment. Because of the other like-minded people doing similar things, which encourages you to do that extra rep, forces you to turn up. Does your environment create accountability? When we are in an office environment, we are in a space of work, where others are also working, which is its own form of accountability. Having a specific person to whom you're accountable also creates a mental environment that is conducive to productivity, where you have no distraction.

53. The four levels of accountability

Once, I would have said that accountability was about setting a task and a deadline and making sure the job was done. The more I work with individuals, the more I see that, depending on where they are at in their journey, the type of accountability they need differs.

I see four levels of accountability:

1. **Level One: Task-focused accountability.** This is the simplest form of accountability. You have a task, for example to write a blog post. You set a deadline, you get the job done. That's it. There's nothing deeper than that, no mindset changes. 'This is what you want to do, this is the deadline, now go and get it done and let me know when you've done it.' Simple, task-focused accountability. A lot of people benefit from this, but sometimes you need something more, a different level of accountability.

2. **Level Two: Goal-focused accountability.** A goal can be broken down into a series of tasks. A goal might be to write a book, launch a podcast or a new product, to get X number of new clients. The accountability at this level is focused around the goal; it's up to you to identify and execute a series of tasks that will enable you to meet the goal. The accountability conversation is about the goal not the tasks, and the support is at that level, so there's less hand holding and more checking in on your progress towards your goal, a reminder of the bigger picture while you're taking those smaller steps.

3. **Level Three: Potential-focused accountability.** This level of accountability is for action-takers, those who would regard themselves as 'busy' but for whatever reason, know they could

be more effective or efficient. Procrastination limits their progress, but not to the level where they're completely disabled. This is about realising potential. You might identify a set of goals that, if achieved, would mean you reach your potential. Again this a different level of accountability conversation; when you're talking about your why, your potential, why haven't you hit it. 'Because I'm not speaking to this person. I'm not launching that product. I'm not opening that business. I'm not doing these posts. I'm not writing those articles.' This level of accountability conversation leaves it up to you to come up with a series of goals, then a series of tasks, to realise the potential that you've identified. Of course you will talk about goals, but not at a detailed level because you're addressing your thinking, your awareness, your understanding of yourself at a higher level, to tap into and engage your potential.

4. **Level Four: Genius-focused accountability.** This is a nudge, perhaps just a five-minute conversation, perhaps a mutual checking in where you say something like, 'You know I've got all these things going on, but I just need to adjust this, tweak that.' It might be a conversation once a week, or once a month; they're just tapping into your genius because they know that you already get it, it's just a reminder, someone to bounce off and keep you motivated and on course.

You might look at these four levels of accountability and wonder which it is that you need. Everybody needs all four, but depending on what stage of your hero's journey you're at, or where you are in your business and life, you might need a different level of accountability. The key is to understand that accountability can take different forms and serve you in different ways.

You might not need your hand held and to be checked in on every day to see if you've completed your tasks. For example in my transformation, the kind of accountability we worked on was about goals and potential. I knew the tasks; I knew how many times I needed to go to the gym; I knew what foods to eat. That wasn't the issue. The issue was, what was my goal for the week (eg to lose X number of pounds) and why was I doing it? What potential was I trying to achieve? I was working toward being photoshoot-ready and reaching a desired level of health. This was what I needed to be held accountable for, where I needed to keep my focus. Then it was up to me to identify and commit to a series of tasks and individual goals.

When you start to understand the different levels of accountability, you can start to understand where you are, what you need and what will be the impact on your life and business. You can then tap into that particular level of accountability.

54. Persistent and consistent actions

Humans generally can be lazy. That's not a bad thing in and of itself. No one wants to work all the time and no one likes to be stressed out. What we want is smarter and more efficient ways to work, and that starts with our actions. Part of playing your A-game is understanding the power of consistent, persistent and intentional actions. There are certain things that always work. If you take certain actions consistently and persistently, something will happen. If you apply a strategy, a bit of skill and knowledge, that 'something' will be something you want. When people don't get what they want, it is because they're not persistent, they're not consistent and they're not diligent enough. What that requires is trust in the process. By trusting the process and the strategy, the outcome will look after itself.

In my time working as a coach, mainly to entrepreneurs and business owners, I have seen a few things that commonly prevent people from taking the actions they need to take. As mentioned earlier on, the big three are procrastination, overwhelm and overthinking.

There is no great secret to consistent, persistent and intentional action. It just requires an understanding of which of the three games for you needs attention, those games being: the inner game (your thoughts, feelings, mindset, attitudes, how you 'turn up' in your head); the game plan (the roadmap, or strategy that you follow to achieve what you're looking for); the outer game (the actions you take). But it's not just about actions. It's about taking it to the next level.

It's persistent and consistent actions that will make the difference. When you do something small, but you do it repeatedly and consistently, without attachment to the outcome, and you keep turning up, you will start to get results. If you are not being consistent, persistent and intentional in your outer game, with your actions, either your inner game is not on point, or you don't have a clear strategy – or both. You can work out which it is using the Change Your Game Scorecard.

CASE STUDY: SIMON THOMAS

Simon Thomas had already been in business for over thirty-five years before we started working together. Simon joined the Change Your Game Accelerator with the aim of learning and adopting new ways to grow his business.

The biggest shift that Simon made was in his mindset, by unlearning some tried and tested growth strategies and adopting new ways of using social media, marketing and sales. Being an engineer, Simon was familiar with new tech innovations, but it's hard to shift your mindset at the speed at which technologies change.

What Simon never did was fail to take action. He was relentlessly consistent. After our coaching sessions, there was never a time where Simon didn't take action – there was always learning, insight and an outcome.

The outcome wasn't always what he wanted, but he always discovered how to do something new, or in a new way.

Being in business for as long as Simon has, it would be so easy to continue taking the same actions, as he was getting good results. But with an openness to change, a desire to improve, and through shifting his mindset and being consistent in his actions, Simon was able to grow his business in the way he wanted and attract new, well-matched clients for his ever-evolving services.

Do you want to up your game? Do you want more success in your life? Do you want to feel that you are making continual, exponential progress? If you commit to one thing after reading this book, commit to being consistent and persistent in just one area and watch the impact this has in every part of your life!

55. The power of transformation

One thing I hugely underestimated was the power of my own transformation on others. When you start to play your game, of course you benefit – you are more disciplined, more focused and you start getting better results in your life. But one thing we underestimate is the intangible effect we have on others.

As I mentioned earlier in this book, in 2018, I decided that I wanted to transform my body. I wanted to lose some weight. I didn't want to just go on a diet, I wanted to change my lifestyle so I could play the game I wanted to play. I had to change the way I thought about health, focus, discipline – everything.

We underestimate the power of making a bold choice, a big decision, of truly playing a game by the rules. When you get educated and informed on what something actually takes, instead of relying on opinion, and you use that empowering information to take action, miracles start to happen.

When you start to play your game, you might think it's quite selfish and all about you. But the thing is, irrespective of whether you're doing this to transform your life or to transform your business, when you focus on you and you get more disciplined, then you get more focused and everybody wins. You win, because you start getting what you want from life, and your clients/customers benefit because they're getting the best version of you. This is where miracles happen.

Winning Each Day, Each Week, Each Month

Now you have the awareness and understanding of how to play your A-game, it's time to get a structure in place that supports you to take consistent action. Imagine winning each moment, each hour, each day, each week, each month. Is this possible? Yes. Is it likely? Probably not.

The key is to have the *intention* of winning each day, with a sound structure in place to facilitate this. Remember:

$$Freedom =$$
$$Focus + Structure + Discipline$$

Where do you need your focus to be each day? What structure will work for you? Where do you need to be disciplined? Only you can answer these honestly.

Below is the structure I use with my clients to set them up to win the month and ultimately win each day.

56. Setting intentions

Each day, instead of setting goals, set intentions. From these intentions, you set your micro goals. Intentions are different to goals in that a goal is an end result, a consequence; an intention is the action and behaviours you're going to take.

Energy flows where intentions are set. Everything is driven by energy and if you set the right intentions with the right mindset, the actions that flow from that can increase your energy. The difference in energy is subtle but significant. By setting out your intentions for each day, you are highlighting the actions you want to take with no attachment to the result. When you set intentions, have in mind what would make you feel that you've had a productive day. Don't overstretch yourself and don't over commit. Focus on two or three intentions to ensure you win the day.

The compound effect of setting and completing intentions each day builds your confidence, builds your momentum, moves the needle on your business and keeps you consistent. This cycle repeats itself. It's a good habit to get into and means the results look after themselves.

57. Micro goals

As we've seen, daily actions are key to changing your game, so setting daily micro goals is essential. Micro goals allow you to take incremental, intentional steps each day that give you a sense of achievement. Micro goals are different to normal goals. Usually, with goals you aim for the stars and if you miss you hit the moon. Micro goals aim for the moon and hit the moon.

Micro goals have specific qualities:

1. **You are in total control**: The bigger goal could be to close two clients, so today's micro goal is to make ten calls. Whatever happens after the tenth call, happens. The micro goal is something you have total control over, regardless of outcome.

2. **They are measurable**: You will never be in any doubt that you have achieved your micro goals. For example, a micro goal could be to write 1,000 words of a book every day. It's not to 'do research for the book', which is too open-ended.

3. **They can be achieved within two hours**: A micro goal should not take up your whole day, but it needs to move you forward, achieve something and make you feel good. This gives you the energy to do the other things you want to do that day.

Being consistent with micro goals means you are likely to achieve more in a week than you would have believed possible.

58. Month by month, week by week, day by day, hour by hour

There is a tendency to overestimate what we can do in a short space of time and underestimate what we can do over a longer period. The structure of setting intentions and micro goals allows you to set some ambitious goals for each month but also not to get overwhelmed by tasks on a day-to-day basis.

I suggest you work in days, weeks and months and, depending on your business model, quarters (three months, or ninety days). You may have plans for one, two or five years and that's fine, but there are so many variables that can impact your long-term plans that it can become overwhelming to think so far ahead.

I recommend you don't look beyond ideally six, maximum twelve, months. This is not to say you shouldn't know what you want to achieve in five years' time, but when thinking about the pragmatic, practical things you want to put in place, you want to think shorter term, things you can execute now.

The best way to apply the structure I suggest below is to ask yourself what success looks like for you either six months or twelve months from now. If you are a business owner, this might relate to level of revenue, number of clients/customers, partnerships – you get the gist. If you are a leader within an organisation, it might be about KPIs. Then, track backwards from this and identify what needs to be in place or achieved in month five or eleven, four or ten, three or nine, in order to hit that target.

To maximise your A-game, you should identify three things for each month:

- A bold outcome
- An essential outcome
- Profile-building actions

Each month, come up with a bold outcome. Something that, if achieved, would be beyond what you could expect. This is not a mission critical outcome, this is an ambitious, perhaps unlikely outcome, but something that excites you and stretches your thinking.

The purpose of setting a bold outcome is to push your comfort zone and test what could be possible. Sometimes our actions are constrained by our limiting beliefs. For the bold outcome, think of your world, a utopia. If there were no limits and you knew it was possible, what bold thing would you aim for this month? This is your opportunity to stretch yourself, to believe in the impossible and set BHAGs (Big Hairy Arse Goals).

These bold outcomes are related to the six- or twelve-month target, but they don't affect the time-scale of the month. If it's achieved, great, ride the wave; if it's not, you don't need to worry, it's not essential.

Essential outcomes are just that: they are essential to you achieving the target you have set for six or twelve months from now. These are the outcomes that keep the momentum going, the things that you must achieve if you're going to reach the target you've set. They give you a framework from which to set your micro goals each day.

When we set targets for the month, we can overstretch ourselves. This is why we are separating bold out-comes and essential outcomes. Setting your essential outcome is about being realistic, pragmatic and hon-est about what you need to and can achieve for the month. Set the essential outcome(s) based on what needs to be in place each month to keep you on sched-ule to meet your six- or twelve-month target.

We live in a time where your profile, whether that of your personal brand or the product/service your business offers, is critical. Profile-building actions are actions that contribute to raising that profile, getting your name out there and building awareness of your brand, product or service. Depending on your target market, who your customers are and your business, where you do this may differ.

One place you can build your profile is social media. If you haven't already, you should identify the best platform or platforms for your sector and register an account to start building your profile. In all of your profile-building actions, focus on what you want to be known for, on adding value and on reaching your target market.

Serve

Now you have the mindset, you have the strategies, and you have the structure to win the month, week and day. You're all set, it's time to play.

The key to playing the A-game is to ensure you are in control of your day more often than you're not. Life will happen and there will always be challenges. When you have control, you will be in a better place to cope with setbacks when life happens.

59. Habits

Show me someone's habits and I will tell you how successful and fulfilled they are. Habits can be good or bad. One of the best books I've read on this is

Atomic Habits by James Clear.[15] In it, he defines habits as, 'The small decisions you make and actions you perform every day.'

The things you do by default each day are all habits. Some have been acquired through social conditioning over many years, others might be more conscious. According to researchers at Duke University, habits account for about 40% of our behaviours on any given day.[16]

Playing your A-game is all about practising good habits, habits that serve you and move you closer to what you are trying to achieve. The concepts, behaviours, strategies and tactics in this book will all help you to form good habits. There are no shortcuts – ultimately, nothing beats consistency and persistency.

The Freedom Formula requires you to form good habits. There is a world full of ideas and projects that never saw the light of day because of a lack of focus, structure and discipline.

60. Radical actions

After reading this book, you might think you need to go away and take big, impressive action. You don't.

---

15 J Clear, *Atomic Habits* (Random House Business, 2018)
16 K Rae Chi, 'Why Are Habits So Hard to Break?' Duke Today (21 January 2016), available at https://today.duke.edu/2016/01/habits

It doesn't need to be dramatic; it's about being smart, consistent and persistent. Radical actions are just that, radical – but they are fully thought out. They make you slightly uncomfortable, they make you feel like you are going against the grain. They feel like actions almost no one would take. But this is exactly right. The A-game is played by only a few, by maybe 5% of people, perhaps only 1%.

This book has been about being focused enough to make radical, smart choices and decisions, to take radical actions to achieve the radical results you want. Keep asking yourself questions each day that push you to take the radical actions you need to take. A great question to ask yourself if you are feeling a little cautious is: what would I do if I *knew* I would succeed?

This is your chance to imagine a utopia, a world where you have no limitations and can play full-out. This question, alongside the intention of taking radical action, will get you the radical results you want.

Summary

With all the recommendations in this book, doing something once won't make a difference. Doing it a few times won't get you the results you want. Doing it when you feel like it won't allow you to reap long-term rewards. The only secret sauce is being consistent and persistent.

To summarise the key learnings of this book:

1. Don't compromise on what you want

2. Embrace all opportunities

3. Respond, don't react

4. Follow the Freedom Formula

5. Don't attach yourself to outcomes

6. Have an intentional mindset

7. Know your values

8. Act like a gold medallist

9. Take persistent and consistent actions

10. Set micro goals

11. Develop habits

Your A-game is your end destination. It's a way of life. Keep practising your habits, maintain your self-awareness and always lean in. If you give up, you are guaranteed to fail. Never give up and you will not fail. Your A-game is the other side of the intentional, radical actions you commit to.

Now is a great time, if you haven't already, to assess how strong your game is currently. I have created a free assessment to determine how effective you are as an entrepreneur and leader.

Visit https://ChangeYourGameScorecard.com to discover your score.

https://changeyourgamescorecard.com/

Now take your first action!

The best way to get to where you want to be is to know *where you are now*.

Go to the link below, take the **Change Your Game Scorecard** and discover how strong your games are.

- Takes less than 4 minutes - and **it's free!** Find out how strong your overall game is.

- Your score can shape your success and up your game.

- You receive a tailored report outlining specific actions for improving your score.

https://ChangeYourGameScorecard.com

The Author

Baiju Solanki is an Award-winning business-man, TEDx speaker and CEO/Founder of EnSpirit Global, a platform that creates next-generation entrepreneurs and business leaders who are ready to grow personally, scale fast and build legacies.

A former Businessman of the Year, Baiju has experience which extends beyond the realm of enterprise. A trained psychologist, lecturer, speaker and author, he supports leaders to realise their own potential and power whilst developing high performance teams around them.

Baiju's experience in academia as a psychology lecturer and in the corporate world as a sales director has helped mould him into the high performance coach whose bold, straight-talking approach helps create radical results for his clients by getting to the roots of the challenges for his clients by going deep!

An inspirational global speaker, Baiju has helped unleash the entrepreneurial spirit and develop thought leaders in the Caribbean, USA to Europe and India.

Baiju is the best selling author of *Change Your Game*, co-author of leadership titles and The EnSpirit Podcast host, and provides value and insights to his followers on all social media platforms.

Baiju is a huge believer that no-one should feel left out. He is actively involved in leadership roles in the sport of cricket and in his local community to foster inclusivity and eliminate discrimination.

https://ChangeYourGameScorecard.com

🌐 www.EnSpirit.Global

🐦 www.twitter.com/EnSpiritGlobal

📷 www.instagram.com/EnSpiritGlobal

📘 www.facebook.com/EnSpiritGlobal

💼 www.linkedin.com/company/EnSpiritGlobal

Or connect with Baiju Solanki at:

- www.BaijuSolanki.com
- www.twitter.com/BaijuSolanki
- www.instagram.com/BaijuSolanki
- www.facebook.com/Baiju.Solanki
- www.linkedin.com/in/baijusolanki